True Murder

Yorkshire Ripper and Fred and Rose West

2 Books in 1

Roger Harrington

Copyright © 2017.

All rights reserved. No part of this publication may be reproduced, distributed, or transmitted in any form or by any means, including photocopying, recording, or other electronic or mechanical methods, without the prior written permission of the publisher, except in the case of brief quotations embodied in critical reviews and certain other noncommercial uses permitted by copyright law.

This book is intended for informational and entertainment purposes only. The publisher limits all liability arising from this work to the fullest extent of the law.

Table of Contents

Introduction
Part 1: Victims
Part 2: Interviews
Part 3: Arrest, Confession & Trial
Part 4: Letters & Audio Tape
Part 5: Psychological Profile
Part 6: Imprisonment & Current Status
Conclusion

Fred & Rose West
Introduction
Early Lives
Midland Road
25 Cromwell Street
Heather West
Investigation
Trial
Aftermath
Conclusion

THE YORKSHIRE RIPPER

Britain's Most Notorious Serial
Killer: Crimes of Pure Evil

Roger Harrington

Introduction

June 2nd, 1946. Peter William Sutcliffe was born to parents Kathleen and John Sutcliffe in the working class area of Bingley, Yorkshire. Considered by both of his parents to be a perfect baby, both his mother and father had their own expectations for what their first-born son was to become in later life. John, his father, wanted Peter to grow up to become a real man's man. A working class; local lad who would enjoy beer, football, weightlifting and an all-round extroverted lifestyle. His mother, Kathleen, had expectations of her son becoming a gentleman. A respectable boy who treated people properly and always made time for others.

To the shock of both of his parents, Peter grew to be neither of these things. As a youngster, he was a quiet, introverted boy. He rarely associated with other children during his primary school years, and instead opted for a more indoor lifestyle. He would spend the majority of his play-time either with his mother or reading books, much to the dismay of his father. By his late childhood years, Peter felt intimidated by his father's brazen masculinity, which forced him to associate more with his mother whom considered Peter her favorite of her six children.

Peter's isolation continues through his primary years into his high school years. As a result of his introverted nature, Peter became a subject of bullying for other children. His weak stature, which Peter's father was particularly disapproving of, made him an easy target for the more burly children to overpower. John Sutcliffe attempted throughout his son's school years to get him to integrate with other children in more physical games but was not successful. Peter's unhappiness in his school life prompted him to regularly play truant from class. It wasn't until his parents were informed of his truancy that they took measures to stop Peter from being bullied.

Peter's bullying soon stopped after this, however the actions served to confirm Peter as someone different. He wasn't like the rest of the children who played sports together or chased after girls. He was considered to be something else entirely.

During Peter's final years of secondary school, he finally attempted to do something about his reputation as an outcast. Peter took up sports and weightlifting in order to get in shape, much to his father's approval. He quickly became stronger and leaner and began to fit in more with the other children in school. Despite this, Peter was terrified of attention being drawn to him in any other aspect of his education. Although he had beefed up physically, his mental state was still solely stuck in its 'introverted' phase.

At age fifteen, Peter Sutcliffe left school and took a string of low-paying, low-skilled, manual labor jobs. He had no real direction as to what he wanted to do for a career. His first job was attained for him by his father, which involved physical labor at a steel mill.

Peter left this job within a few weeks and took up an apprenticeship in engineering, which he also quit less than a year later. He then took to doing more manual labor in a factory, and again, left within a few months' time.

Throughout all this time, the relationship between Peter and his mother remained strong. He spent a large portion of his free time with her and did whatever she would ask of him. In contrast, Peter's relationship with his father suffered as both grew older. Peter considered his father's increasing absence away from their family due to his love of sport and socializing was unfair on everyone else. Although their relationship rekindled slightly during Peter's late teenage years due to his sudden enthusiasm for weightlifting and male-oriented activities, this was only short-lived. John Sutcliffe's biggest concern regarding his son's dissimilar characteristics was that he rarely showed interest in the opposite sex.

In 1966, at the age of twenty, Sutcliffe approach a young lady named Sonia Szurma while out with friends a hotel bar. Sonia would be Sutcliffe's first and only consensual partner throughout his entire life, and would later become his wife. By 1973, Sutcliffe had secured himself a steady job (the first one of his life) at Britannia Works of Anderton International. Soon, the pressures from both his and Sonia's family for the pair to wed finally coerced Peter into asking Sonia to marry him. They married in August 1974, and because of their financial struggles, were forced to live with Sonia's parents until they could find their own home.

During his early twenties, Peter Sutcliffe began working as a Gravedigger in Bingley Cemetery. It was around this time that friends of Peter notice that his sense of humor began to take on a more sinister tone. Peter's friend Gary Jackson, who worked with Peter during his stint as a gravedigger, told of the enjoyment Peter got from playing 'pranks' with the skeletons he was entrusted to bury. Peter would also remove jewellery from the corpses passed to him in order to sell on; something which was highly frowned upon and considered to be very disrespectful. It would be Sutcliffe's repeated lateness and general deadbeat attitude which caused him to lose this job.

In February 1975, Peter left his manual labor role at Britannia Works of Anderton International and soon took up a role as a HGV driver for T&WH Clark Holdings Ltd in Bradford; an occupation which would later become synonymous with his crimes. He held this position for the rest of his free life.

By his late twenties, Sutcliffe was considered to be a hard-working husband who kept himself to himself. On the surface, he showed no signs of violence and played the part of the loving husband whenever possible. He had a handful of close friends, one of which was his brother-in-law Robin Holland. He and Robin drank together for a number of years until Peter's strange behavior became too much for him. Peter regularly boasted about his exploits with the local prostitutes to Robin, while at the same time offer grandiose statements regarding the wrongdoings of men who regularly cheat on their wives.

Peter continued this confusing, hypocritical stance on infidelity until it became too much for Robin, who cut contact with Peter around the mid-1970s. It was around this time that Peter and his wife were to inform their families of the terrible news regarding their desire for children: they were unable to conceive naturally. Sonia had suffered multiple miscarriages throughout her relationship with Peter, resulting in the eventual confirmation that she would be unable to bear full-term pregnancy. This was a devastating blow for the pair as they both desperately wanted children.

Another of Peter's close friends, Trevor Birdsall, who was a close confidant of Peter's during his traumatic period regarding multiple miscarriages, remained in contact with Peter right up until his arrest in 1981, despite the strange and often shocking statements Peter's would make in his presence.

This bizarre side of Peter Sutcliffe was only seen by these two people: Robin Holland Trevor Birdsall. To everyone else, he was an everyday, working class gentleman who could do no harm to anyone.

Peter Sutcliffe would later come to be known as the Yorkshire Ripper; the man who terrorized the north of England in a series of vicious killings spanned six years.

Part 1: Victims

"Stone-In-Sock" Attack (Survived)

Before progressing to murder, Sutcliffe carried out a string of violent attacks on women which many survived. In fact, Sutcliffe has been confirmed to have carried out 23 attacks in total, of which 10 survived the ordeal. This places him in a unique category of serial killer as he has an almost equal ratio of survived victims to murdered victims.

Peter's first known attack came in September 1969. A few weeks prior to this attack, Sutcliffe had spotted his wife Sonia out with another man; a local ice-cream salesman. Sutcliffe, feeling completely dejected, confronted Sonia regarding her actions. She refused to answer any of his questions, leaving their relationship in a state of turmoil.

Sutcliffe, in an act of revenge, elicited the services of a local prostitute (her name remains unknown). He found in a local petrol station and after negotiating with her, they decided on the standard price of £5. However, when the time came, Sutcliffe felt awash with guilt and disgust. By his own admission he realized "what a vulgar and disgusting person she was. I tried to wriggle out of the situation but I felt stupid."

Sutcliffe realized that he'd given the lady a £10 instead of £5. He confessed to her that he had changed his mind and they agreed that they would go back to the garage he picked her up from, drop her off, and she could keep the £5. She would get Sutcliffe's change and then the incident would be over.

Much to Sutcliffe's annoyance, the prostitute went back into the garage he had met her and refused to come out. He then realized that the men who worked in the garage were the prostitute's 'protectors' and that they wouldn't give him back his money. By this point, Sutcliffe was feeling increasingly ashamed. One of the prostitute's protectors came out and threatened Sutcliffe with a wrench, causing him to flee.

To add insult to injury, the woman soon reappeared with a different man. By Sutcliffe's accounts, he was a "big-built bloke. They walked off together, having a laugh. I just felt stupid. I drove home angry, outraged, embarrassed and humiliated. I felt a hatred for [the prostitute] and her kind."

Several weeks later, Sutcliffe again saw the same woman in Lumb Lane pub. He approached her and told her that she could "put things right". However, the prostitute thought this was simply a joke. She would go on to tell everyone in the pub about Sutcliffe's antics, embarrassing him further.

The "stone-in-sock" attack would come as a direct result of Sutcliffe's sheer embarrassment from the money incident. Peter and his friend Trevor Birdsall were scouting the streets for reasons unknown to Birdsall. Sutcliffe wanted to find the prostitute who wronged him one last time, but didn't inform Birdsall of his true motivations. Sutcliffe was unable to find her, but at one point, Sutcliffe suddenly jumped out of their vehicle and ran out of sight.

He returned ten minutes later and, according to Birdsall, was out of breath and showed signs of exhaustion. He asked Trevor to "drive off quickly." Once they were out of the area, Sutcliffe claimed that he had followed a woman into her house and attacked her with a stone in a sock. A sock he then took out of his pocket and discarded out of the window.

Fortunately, the prostitute survived the attack and was able to give the police details regarding the vehicle Sutcliffe had disappeared into. Peter was visited by the police in relation to the attack but was not arrested. Sutcliffe would later claim that:

"I was out of my mind with the obsession of finding this prostitute [the one who stole his money]. It was getting late. I just gave vent to my anger on the first one I saw."

Anna Rogulskyj (Survived)

On the morning of July 5th 1975, Peter Sutcliffe would carry out his second attack. It had been almost six years since Sutcliffe had carried out his previous attack on an unknown prostitute, and reasons for his cooling-off period are widely theorized. He may have committed crimes during this lull, however no such incidents are on official record. His next confirmed attack came on Anna Rogulskyj, a 36 year old prostitute.

Sutcliffe and Rogulskyj had previously met at least twice before, although there is no confirmation that anything happened between them. On the night of July 4th 1975, Sutcliffe had driven into Keighley. Rogulskyj had been out drinking that same night and was returning to her boyfriend's house sometime before midnight. As she headed back to his place, a voice perked up from behind her asking if she was available for business. Rogulskyj rejected the person's advances and quickened her pace to her boyfriend's house.

Unfortunately, Rogulskyj's boyfriend didn't answer the door to her, forcing her to turn around and head back the way she came; through a deserted alleyway. The same man would ask her again if she wanted business but again she rejected him. The man was Sutcliffe, and in a fit of rage, attacked Rogulskyj with a ball-peen hammer from behind.

He hit her three times in the head in order to subdue her. Once she was disoriented, Sutcliffe pushed her to the ground, lifted up her dress and attempted to slash her abdomen with a small penknife. His actions were disturbed by a nearby neighbor inquiring as to what the commotion was, causing Sutcliffe to flee the scene. Despite his intentions, he left Rogulskyj alive. He would later say that he "intended to kill her but was disturbed," along with "I didn't mean her to suffer. I meant her to die." Two statements which are very revealing into Sutcliffe's initial motivations to kill.

Peter then returned home to his wife and joined her in bed. Anna Rogulskyj miraculously survived her attack, although recent statements from her claim that she wish she hadn't. Her incident with Sutcliffe has forced her into a life of isolation. Rogulskyj rarely leaves the house anymore. She lives alone and has a house barricaded with intruder alarms and sensors. She is terrified of the dark, shadows and strangers. She received a large payout from the Criminal Compensation Board, however she claims it can't give her back the life she's lost.

Olive Smelt (Survived)

On August 15th 1975, Peter Sutcliffe attacked 46 year old office cleaner Olive Smelt in Halifax. Olive's usual Fridays consisted of a few drinks with friends at her local pub the Royal Oak before heading home to her husband and family.

The same night, Peter Sutcliffe and Trevor Birdsall were also making their way round the Halifax pubs, eventually ending up in the Royal Oak. Birdsall recalls Sutcliffe remarking that the place was a "prostitute's pub" and singled-out Olive Smelt as an obvious "worker".

Sutcliffe made comments to Smelt as he passed her at the bar, however Smelt responded to his accusations with force, promptly putting Sutcliffe in his place. This may have been the trigger which cemented Smelt's status as a Yorkshire Ripper victim, as the embarrassment he felt surely reminded him of his previous humiliating instances.

Once the pub had shut, Sutcliffe and Birdsall left and drove towards Bradford. On the way there, Sutcliffe requested that Trevor slow the car down as he recognized Smelt as she was walking home. He exited the car, and as Birdsall recalls, Sutcliffe walked the opposite direction to the way Smelt was going. In reality, Sutcliffe was heading off Smelt in an alleyway from the opposite direction. As he approached her, Sutcliffe remarked to her about the weather, and once she had sufficiently passed him, he turned around and hit her in the head with a hammer.

Once she was subdued, Sutcliffe attempted to slash Smelt's buttocks with a knife but was disturbed by an oncoming vehicle. He quickly fled the scene back to the safety of his vehicle and his friend. Birdsall reclaimed that Sutcliffe was "unusually quiet" at this point. Sutcliffe simply claimed that he had been "talking to a woman".

Sutcliffe later revealed in his confession statements that he had fully intended to kill Olive Smelt but again, was disturbed by a passer-by. Additionally, Trevor Birdsall read in the following day's newspaper of Smelt's brutal attack, and even suspected Sutcliffe as the potential culprit. However, he did nothing regarding his assumptions.

Olive Smelt was discovered in the alleyway she was attacked soon after Sutcliffe had fled. She survived her ordeal. However, another woman's life was ruined by Sutcliffe's actions.

Tracy Browne (Survived)

Only 14 years old at the time of her attack, Tracy Browne was to be Peter Sutcliffe's youngest victim. On August 27th 1975, twelve days after Sutcliffe's attack on Olive Smelt, Sutcliffe approached Browne as she walked home from visiting a friend. Browne had told her parents she was to be home for 10:30pm and was running late. She possibly believed that Sutcliffe could offer her a lift home.

The two talked as they walked through Keighley (in the same location Sutcliffe had attacked Anna Rogulskyj), with Sutcliffe occasionally hanging back to either "blow his nose" or "tie his shoelace". Once they had reached the gate to the farmhouse where Browne lived, Sutcliffe suddenly attacked Browne from behind. He hit her with a hammer, but yet again, was disturbed by a passing car. Before he fled, he managed to throw Browne's body over a fence and into a bush in order to keep her hidden while he escaped.

Luckily, Tracy Browne survived her attack. She was able to give a detailed photo-fit of her attacker to police which greatly resembled Peter Sutcliffe. Despite this, the links between the Ripper's previous crimes and this one were never made by the Yorkshire Police due to the severe age difference between Browne and all previous victims.

This was a notable point of controversy which would later come back to haunt the Yorkshire Police in their investigation. Tracy Browne and her mother even went to Keighley police station to make an official statement regarding Browne's attacker being the Ripper, but were simply laughed at and told to leave. Browne's father would later say that if the police had taken his daughter's claims seriously, some of the Yorkshire Ripper's victims would still be alive.

Sutcliffe himself did not accept responsibility for this attack until 1992, possibly out of embarrassment that he had attacked a minor.

Sutcliffe's rage during this period was also increasing. So far, he had attacked three women within six weeks and was unable to successfully kill any of them. His failure at even being a serial killer was becoming evident. He already felt a sense of shame and humiliation about himself, and being unable to carry out his true intentions only infuriated him further.

Wilma McCann

October 30th 1975. Wilma McCann's body was discovered at 7:41am by a local milkman. Her trousers had been dropped to her knees and her clothes had been removed to expose her body. Blood had soaked into her hair and mutilations were present on her stomach, neck and chest. Wilma McCann was the first victim of the Yorkshire Ripper.

Wilma McCann was 28 year old prostitute and mother of four. On the night of her death, she had kissed goodnight to her children and left for the pubs in the Chapeltown area of Leeds. She visited multiple clubs and bars between the hours of 8pm and 1am, consuming around 14 measures of spirits in that time. She was last seen around 1am.

McCann attempted to solicit a lift from someone back to her home due to her being worse for wear. Unfortunately for her, one of the people she attempted to thumb down was Peter Sutcliffe who was driving through Leeds for work. Sutcliffe pulled over and picked up McCann, who promptly asked Sutcliffe if he "wanted business". Sutcliffe initially responded with hesitation, to which McCann coerced him to the point that he agreed.

Sutcliffe drove them to a desolate area near Prince Phillip Playing Fields, very close to McCann's home. Sutcliffe still remained reluctant, telling McCann that he found it difficult to become aroused instantly. McCann then became abusive and stormed off. Sutcliffe managed to talk her round to having sex on the playing field. He lay his coat down for her, concealing his hammer underneath it. When McCann sat down, he suddenly attacked her from behind. He struck in the head several times. Sutcliffe then went to a toolbox he kept in the back of his vehicle and took out a knife. He went back to her dying body and lacerated her stomach, neck and lungs.

Sutcliffe claims that he felt remorse at this point. He claims to have spent the hours following his murder of Wilma McCann in a haze. Although, contradictory, he later claims that the McCann incident was the one which "started it all off".

By this point, there were 150 police officers working to track down the man who would come to be known as the Yorkshire Ripper. In total, seven thousand householders had been interviewed regarding all previous attacks and a further three hundred from anyone connected to Wilma McCann. As would become a recurring theme in the Yorkshire Ripper investigation, the police were no closer to finding the culprit.

Emily Jackson

Peter Sutcliffe would go eighty days without lashing out again. On January 20th 1976, 42 year old part-time prostitute Emily Jackson would be the Ripper's second murdered victim.

Although Jackson held a common office job by day, she had taken to picking up men of an evening in order to make some extra cash. Her usual method of picking up clients was to cruise around local pubs during closing hours and take men back to their vehicles for "business".

Around 7pm on January 20th, Jackson came into contact with Peter Sutcliffe at the Gaiety pub in Leeds. They agreed on a price of £5 and went with Sutcliffe into his vehicle. He drove them around half a mile away from the pub to an isolated area away from prying eyes, when he stopped and said that there was a problem with his car's engine. Jackson offered her assistance in fixing the engine, and used her cigarette lighter so that Sutcliffe could check under the car's bonnet.

As she held her head low against the car, Sutcliffe struck her twice with his hammer, causing her to collapse to the ground. He dragged Jackson's body into a nearby junkyard and removed her clothing. He took out a screwdriver, a deviation from his usual implement of choice, and brutally stabbed Jackson a total of 52 times across her neck, breasts, stomach and back. He left her for dead.

Sutcliffe later remarked that he felt a "seething hatred" for Emily Jackson due to the overbearing, cheap perfume she was wearing. Sutcliffe blames his first murder of Wilma McCann as the event which instilled in him a compulsion to murder again. He said that the first murder had "unhinged him completely" and was now powerless to control himself.

Sutcliffe additionally mutilated Jackson's body post-death in order to satisfy the rage he felt. He stomped on Jackson's right thigh hard enough to leave the impression of his boot in her skin. He also stuffed a wooden plank between Jackson's legs post-death, possibly as a final act of humiliation.

When Jackson's body was discovered the following morning, the police instantly linked it with the previous death of Wilma McCann. They were now developing a picture of the man responsible: he was around thirty years of age, bulky, had dark hair and facial hair, size 8-9 boot, didn't kill for financial purposes and harbored a deep resentment of women.

Marcella Claxton (Survived)

In the early hours of the morning on May 9th 1976, Marcella Claxton was walking home from a friends' party in Chapeltown, Leeds. Claxton, a 20-year-old prostitute was approached a man in a large white car who pulled up alongside her. The man in the car was the Yorkshire Ripper.

Despite Claxton not working that evening, she was happy to ask for a lift from the driver. Sutcliffe offered Claxton £5 in order to have sex with him, but Claxton refused his offer. Claxton then left his vehicle in order to urinate, although details of what exactly happened at this point are contradictory. Sutcliffe claims that Claxton was willing to engage in sex, whereas Claxton claims that she simply left to urinate and not to engage in sex. Regardless, as Claxton exited

Sutcliffe's vehicle, she heard a clang on the other side of the car.

Sutclife claimed that it was simply his wallet he had dropped, however in actual fact it was his intended murder weapon. As Claxton turned around to urinate, Sutcliffe approached her and delivered eight or nine vicious blows to her head with his ball-peen hammer. Sutcliffe, uncharacteristically, didn't stick around despite there being no one else nearby. He did not inflict any stabbing wounds to Claxton and instead simply drove off at speed.

Claxton survived her attack. She managed to stagger to a nearby phone box to ring for help. As she sat on the floor of the phone box awaiting an ambulance, Claxton claims that Sutcliffe came back to look for her:

"A man in a white car kept driving past. He seemed to be staring and looking for me. It was the man that hurt me. He got out and began searching the spot where he had left me. He must have come back to finish me off."

This is a further point which is left open for discussion as Sutcliffe also denies he did this. Additionally, Claxton claims that Sutcliffe attempted to masturbate onto her as she lay on the floor, although this is also denied by Sutcliffe. It is important to note that Marcella Claxton was the only victim of the Ripper to be of African descent. At the time, race was a prominent issue amongst the working class, and even the Leeds police were said to have made derogatory claims regarding Marcella Claxton's intellectual capabilities.

Irene Richardson

It would be 271 days before the Yorkshire Ripper claimed his next victim. 28-year-old prostitute Irene Richardson was murdered in the exact location as Sutcliffe's previous failed murder attempt, Marcella Claxton. The murder of Irene Richardson marks a vital escalation point in the Ripper's modus operandi.

February 5th, 1977. Irene Richardson had found herself broke and, despite warnings of the Ripper amongst prostitutes, found herself hanging on street corners alone. The same night, Peter Sutcliffe was trawling the streets of Leeds in his Ford Corsair when he came across Richardson.

Near to the Gaiety pub (where the Ripper had met previous victim Emily Jackson), Richardson approached Sutcliffe herself without prompt. She jumped in to his vehicle, despite Sutcliffe telling her that he wasn't interested in her wares. Richardson managed to talk Sutcliffe around, promising him a "good time".

Sutcliffe agreed and drove them to the same spot he had attacked Marcella Claxton nine months previous. Upon leaving their car to have sex on the grass, Peter concealed his usual murder weapons into his pocket. Richardson decided to urinate on the grass before they went ahead with their business, to which Sutcliffe attacked her in his usual manner. He delivered three harsh blows to her head with a hammer, with one particular strike which drove fragments of Richardson's skull into her brain. Once she was incapacitated, Sutcliffe ripped open her blouse and repeatedly stabbed her torso with a Stanley knife.

Sutcliffe quickly made his getaway after being disturbed by nearby voices. Before he left the scene, however, Sutcliffe covered Richardson's lower body with her coat; a method of either theatrics or making it seems to passers-by as though she was merely a sleeping drunkard.

Sutcliffe had unknowingly made a vital error at this point. He had driven his Ford Corsair onto the mud of the field he murdered Richardson on. This was enough for the police to ascertain the tyres the vehicle had as well as the make and model of the vehicle.

Sutcliffe would later go on to say:

"By this time, after Richardson killing, prostitutes became an obsession with me and I couldn't stop myself, it was like some sort of a drug.

Patricia Atkinson

76 days after the murder of Irene Richardson, Sutcliffe struck again. His next victim, 32-year-old Patricia Atkinson would

be very revealing of the Yorkshire Ripper's true intentions.

On April 23rd 1977, Sutcliffe had been driving through Manningham for work when he spotted Atkinson stumbling along the late night streets, clearly intoxicated. She was being loud and brash, shouting obscenities in the streets and banging on car windows. Without any prompt, Atkinson entered Sutcliffe's vehicle. She told him that they could go back to her flat which was about a five minute drive away.

They entered Atkinson's flat in Oak Lane, Manningham. Almost immediately, Sutcliffe pulled out a hammer he had concealed in his coat and delivered four brutal blows to the back of Atkinson's head. She instantly fell to the floor, leaving spatters of blood throughout her flat. He hit her once more while she was grounded, then picked up her lifeless body and placed her on her bed.

Sutcliffe exposed Atkinson's chest and genitals. He then slashed her in his usual manner; forceful thrusts into her stomach and back with a knife, as well as cuts to the side of her body. Additionally, Sutcliffe performed an act of mutilation he had never done before (and never did again): he scraped at her torso with the claw end of his hammer, possibly as an experiment.

Sutcliffe noticed that Atkinson was still alive; however he didn't consciously finish her off. Instead, he left her flat as she was still making "gurgling noises", fully confident she would not recover.

This incident marks the only time that a Ripper victim was murdered indoors. The murder of Patricia Atkinson also bears resemblance to Jack the Ripper's final murder 90 years previous. In both cases the culprits were sexual sadists who achieved heightened sensations upon murdering and mutilating women, and both killed the majority of their victims outdoors. However, when the opportunity of killing indoors presented itself, both "Rippers" performed acts which they had never carried out previously. Jack the Ripper mutilated his indoor victim Mary Jane Kelly to a degree which, even by today's standards, is considered horrific. And the Yorkshire

Ripper adopted a strange 'clawing' method of mutilation on Patricia Atkinson, something which was never seen in his method of killing before or ever again. This indicates that Peter Sutcliffe desired more than to simply 'hit and run' as he did with so many victims, and, if given the opportunity, would have performed more severe disfigurements to all who he killed. The privacy offered by such circumstances would allow him to act out his fantasies in full.

Jayne MacDonald

16-year-old Jayne MacDonald was to be the Ripper's first 'innocent' victim. She had only just left school and had no intentions of becoming a sex worker

On June 26th 1977, Jayne MacDonald had been out with friends in Leeds city center. She had met a boy she liked there named Mark Jones whom she walked back to her area with. She and Mark parted ways near St James Hospital and MacDonald made her way to a nearby taxi rank.

Unfortunately, the taxi rank was closed so MacDonald was forced to walk back to her home at Scott Hall Avenue (the same street where the first Ripper victim Wilma McCann lived). On the same evening, Peter Sutcliffe had been out drinking in Bradford with his friends Ronald and David Barker. He dropped them both off at their home which happened to be on the same street he lived, but instead of going home, Sutcliffe turned his car around and headed back to Leeds to look for his next victim.

It was around 2am when Sutcliffe noticed Jayne MacDonald walking along Chapeltown Road in Leeds. He observed her for a while, making sure no one else was in the vicinity before concealing his hammer and knife in his coat pocket. He silently followed her for a few minutes and noticed that she didn't once turn round to look at him.

Sutcliffe blitz attacked MacDonald from behind as she passed through a playground in Reginald Street. He struck her in the back of the head and she instantly fell to the floor. He dragged her further into the playground so they were securely isolated, and then beat her again. He pulled up her clothes, stabbed in the chest and back with his knife and left her for dead.

The following day, upon hearing the news of Jayne MacDonald's murder, reports say that Sutcliffe suffered genuine distress at the fact she wasn't a prostitute as he had previously assumed. Sutcliffe later claimed:

"When I saw in the papers that MacDonald was so young and not a prostitute, I felt like someone inhuman and I realized that it was a devil driving me against my will and that I was a beast. When the Ripper came up in conversation at work or in a pub I was able to detach my mind from the fact that it was me they were talking about, and I was able to discuss it normally. This amazed me at times that I was able to do this."

Sutcliffe is likely telling the truth in this statement. It wouldn't be a stretch for him to feel distressed at the fact he had deviated from his preferred victim type. The implications of his actions would be that he was not fulfilling his desired fantasy, meaning the murder would be a 'waste'. Serial killers, especially those as disorganized as the Yorkshire ripper, are also able to consciously disassociate themselves from their actions, especially if they have performed acts which even they themselves feel ashamed of.

Although Sutcliffe's claims of remorse at this point may have been genuine, it would be impossible for someone as deluded, sociopathic and impulsive as him to maintain this level of guilt.

Maureen Long (Survived)

Only two weeks later would come Sutcliffe's next attack. The circumstances regarding the attack on 42-year-old prostitute Maureen Long echo those of his previous victim Jayne MacDonald.

Long had been out drinking in Bradford with friends on the night of July 9th 1977. She was heading back to her husband's home (although they were separated) at around 2am. Similarly, Sutcliffe had been out drinking with his friends Ronnie and David Barker the same night. He dropped them off home, then turned around and headed out to hunt for his next victim.

Sutcliffe noticed Long as she was walking alone through Bradford city center. He approached her from his vehicle and asked her if she was "going far". Long asked Sutcliffe whether that was his way of offering her a lift, to which he replied he was. She got in his vehicle and told Sutcliffe to head towards the area of Bowling where she lived.

Bizarrely, Sutcliffe took Long the entire way to her house. Long told him to stop at the end of the street so that she could check if her husband was home. He was, so Long suggested to Sutcliffe that they go to an alleyway to perform their "business". They settled on an alleyway near her home.

Long got out of Sutcliffe's vehicle to urinate once they had reached their destination, which is when Sutcliffe took the opportunity to strike. As she was crouching, he struck the back of her head with his hammer. She fell down. Sutcliffe then dragged her into an area of nearby wasteland and stabbed her in the stomach in his usual method of killing. He then left her bleeding out on the floor.

The following day, Sutcliffe was "shocked" to discover that Maureen Long had survived his attacks. His nervousness grew as he believed Long would be able to identify him due to the amount of time they spent together. However, Sutcliffe felt a wave of relief when he discovered Long was a sufferer of amnesia and was unable to recall what he looked like.

Jean Jordan

Serial killers often expand their murders to other territories once they realize that authorities are aware of their actions. While the Ripper was fully aware that the regions of Bradford and Leeds knew of his existence, he did not branch out to different areas until his sixth kill. Sutcliffe himself later claimed that: "I realized things were hotting up a bit in Leeds and Bradford. People had dubbed me the Ripper. I decided to go to Manchester to kill a prostitute"

Jean Jordan, a 20-year-old prostitute from Manchester was working her usual locations on the night of October 1st 1977. Sutcliffe had become familiar with Manchester during his drinking trips there with Ronnie and David Barker, particularly the red-light districts. Sutcliffe had also recently acquired a new vehicle, a red Ford Corsair, due to his old vehicle being so heavily involved with most of his previous attacks.

Sutcliffe noticed Jordan at around 9pm. He saw her haggling with another client before she noticed Sutcliffe looking. She was about to get in with him but changed her mind at the last moment. Something which Sutcliffe referred to as "the biggest mistake she ever made". Sutcliffe and Jordan agreed on the standard price of £5, and drove out to a deserted grassy wasteland near Southern Cemetery in Manchester.

As they left the car and walked into the shrubbery, Sutcliffe pulled out the hammer he had concealed in his coat. He delivered eleven brutal blows to Jordan's head from behind, causing her to fall into the bushes, screaming. As Jordan moaned, Sutcliffe heard the sounds of nearby voices. It would appear that he and Jordan weren't the only couple in the area. He held his hand over Jordan's mouth to silence her and dragged her further into the woodland. While crouching down with her, he saw a car's headlights in the distance. Sutcliffe feared he had been caught, causing him to quickly discard Jordan's body and rush into his car.

Sutcliffe drove off in haste, but realised on his journey that he had made a grave error: he had given Jean Jordan the money in advance and hadn't taken it back. The £5 was also a newly-minted note, meaning there was a high likelihood it could be traced back to him. Sutcliffe decided to wait it out and possibly return at a later date to claim it back.

For the next few days, no newspapers mentioned the murder of Jean Jordan at all. Luckily, Sutcliffe had left her in a location only frequented at night, so there was little chance of anyone discovering her body. After a week, Sutcliffe took the risk of heading back to the crime scene in order to reclaim his money.

On October 9th, Sutcliffe returned to the site after attending a party with his parents. He dropped them off at their home in Bradford then made the trip to Manchester. Sutcliffe discovered Jordan's body in the same place he had left it. However, he was unable to find the £5 note. He checked all of Jordan's pockets, handbag and the whole area where her and Sutcliffe had been but to no avail.

In a fit of rage brought on by being unable to find the only piece of physical evidence he'd overlooked so far, Sutcliffe brutally attacked Jordan's corpse with a knife he had brought with him. He viciously attacked her entire body, eventually causing her stomach to explode due to the force of his lacerations. He then picked up a piece of discarded glass and stabbed at her until he exhausted himself. Eventually, Sutcliffe made the decision to cut off Jean Jordan's head. The piece of glass he had previously used was inadequate for such a task, despite his efforts. He then returned to his car, picked up a hacksaw and tried with that instead, but again was unsuccessful. Finally accepting defeat, Sutcliffe kicked at Jordan's body to vent his excess rage and returned home, distressed. Sutcliffe later claimed that his motivation for removing the head of Jean Jordan was to "create a mystery about it".

Given the evidence he had left behind, as well as spending a large chunk of time at the crime scene allowing possible witnesses to see him, Sutcliffe was convinced that his run would soon come to an end. The morning after Sutcliffe's re-visit to Jordan's crime scene, her body was discovered and police were alerted. Sure enough, the £5 note was found by police in a hidden compartment in Jordan's handbag. However, so much time had elapsed between her death and the discovery of her body that it was impossible to narrow down the suspects based on the note alone.

Marilyn Moore (Survived)

It would be 73 days later that 25-year-old prostitute Marilyn Moore would be attacked by the Yorkshire Ripper.

December 14th 1977. Moore was doing her usual business in Chapeltown, Leeds when Sutcliffe noticed her. He had previously seen Moore refuse to get into a car with a potential client, instilling the idea in him that Moore was perhaps very picky with who she did business with. In order to make himself appear 'safe', Sutcliffe made sure that Moore heard him shouting "see you later, take care!" to an imaginary person as she passed by. They struck up conversation and agreed on a price of £5 for Moore's services.

They drove around half a mile away. Sutcliffe told Moore that his name was Dave, something which he had never done before and was a rare deviation from his modus operandi. It was a sign that Sutcliffe was becoming more aware of the notoriety surrounding the Ripper. He was adapting his methodology to the circumstances, something uncommon for a killer as disorganized as Sutcliffe.

They found themselves near Prince Philip Playing Fields, the same spot where Sutcliffe murdered Wilma McCann two years before. Sutcliffe suggested they move to the back of his car, and when Moore turned her back, Sutcliffe attempted to blitz attack her from behind but lost his balance. He only managed to graze her, to which Moore screamed out for help. He hit her again several more times, while calling Moore a "filthy prostitute bitch". She gradually fell into unconsciousness, but her screams had alerted the attention of nearby neighbors. Sutcliffe quickly made haste, leaving Moore on the roadside as he sped away.

Moore regained her composure and managed to make her way to a nearby phone box to call for help. She was soon taken to

Leeds Infirmary for emergency care. She survived was the seventh person to survive a Ripper attack.

The attack on Moore provided the Yorkshire Police with proof that this was a Ripper-related incident. The tyre tracks found near the crime scene matched the ones found at Irene Richardson's murder site. Additionally, Marilyn Moore was able to provide a detailed photo-fit of her assailant, but due to her head injuries, police did not take her word as seriously as they should have.

Yvonne Pearson

By January 1978, Yorkshire Police believed that the terrorizing spree of the Yorkshire

Ripper was over, perhaps discouraged by his recent unsuccessful attack on Marilyn Moore. Modern criminal profiling methods would tell us that such a killer would never stop killing until death or imprisonment intervened, however, what police also didn't know was that the Ripper had already attacked again. The body would not be found until two months later.

21-year-old prostitute Yvonne Pearson was out on business on the night of January 21st 1978. Her local haunt was the Lumb Lane area of Bradford, which Sutcliffe also found himself in that same evening. Pearson approached Sutcliffe by tapping on the window of his red Ford Corsair. They quickly agreed on their price and Sutcliffe drove them both to an area of wasteland behind Drummond's Mill (where Sutcliffe's father worked at the time).

They planned to have sex on the floor outside of Sutcliffe's vehicle. When Pearson exited the car, Sutcliffe used the opportunity to strike her several times in her head with a wailing hammer which he kept concealed under his seat. While Pearson was disoriented, another car pulled up right next to Sutcliffe's. Luckily, he was able to hide her body behind a discarded sofa in the wasteland area, and managed to silence her long enough until the car disappeared.

Sutcliffe claimed that it "felt like hours" as he lay hidden with Pearson's spasming body, although in actuality it was only a few minutes. Finally alone, Sutcliffe exposed

Pearson and, in a deviation from his usual method of killing, kicked her until she passed out. He felt a growing rage inside him due to nearly being caught, and was acting out the only way he knew how.

Sutcliffe hid Pearson's body by covering her with soil and discarded items he found in the waste site. He then decided to place the sofa on top of her so that no one would be able to see her body from the road.

Pearson was not discovered until March 26th 1978, a whole two months and five days after the murder took place. Although on the surface, Pearson's wounds did not bear the hallmarks of a Sutcliffe's previous attacks, the arrangement of her clothing was indicative that this was indeed a Ripper murder.

It is interesting to note that, upon the discovery of Pearson's body, a copy of the Daily Mirror dated February 21st (one month after the murder took place) was found less than one of her arms. Sutcliffe later denied ever re-visiting the crime scene of Yvonne Pearson and the police have no reason to doubt his claims. This remains the only real unsolved mystery in the entire case of the Yorkshire Ripper.

Helen Rytka

Ten days after the murder of Yvonne Pearson, Sutcliffe would kill again. This time, he would expand his territory further. Due to the growing concern amongst prostitutes in Yorkshire, as well as the established Ripper murder in Manchester, he decided to claim his next victim in Huddersfield.

18-year-old prostitute Helen Rytka was new to the sex worker industry. She had only been in the trade a few weeks when Sutcliffe approached her on the evening of January 31st 1978.

Sutcliffe's plan of attack for this kill was to suggest they move to the back of the car, then attack when his target's back was turned. However, in an unexpected turn of events, Sutcliffe became aroused when the time came to perform the deed with Rytka. He used the ruse anyway, but due to his obvious arousal, Sutcliffe was unable to deliver his hammer blow with enough force to incapacitate her. He only grazed Rytka's head, to which she pleaded with him to stop, but Sutcliffe attacked her two more times causing her to fall to the ground.

Despite Sutcliffe not being familiar with the area he was in, he dragged Rytka to the closest isolated area he could find. It was a wood-yard in Great Northern Street. He waited until Rytka's moans subsided and, while covering her mouth with his hand and telling her she "would be alright", Sutcliffe lay on top of Rytka and had sex with her. Of all the Yorkshire Ripper's many attacks, Helen Rytka was the only one he actually slept with.

Once the deed was done, Sutcliffe returned to his vehicle to pick up his knife and hammer. When he returned, he beat Rytka until she was unconscious and stabbed her in the lungs and heart. He disposed of her possessions on his route home, and hid Rtyka's body behind a stack of wood. She would be discovered three days later.

Vera Millward

It would be three and a half months before the Yorkshire Ripper would strike again. This time, it was 40-year-old prostitute Vera Millward.

Sutcliffe again made his way to Manchester for Millward's murder on the night of Tuesday, May 16th 1978. His motivations for this particular location are unknown, but it had been over 7 months since the murder of Jean Jordan in Manchester, so he possibly figured that awareness of his crimes in this area had died down enough to comfortably strike again.

On Tuesdays, Vera Millward had a regular client who picks her up from outside her flat in Greenham Avenue. Unfortunately, he did not show up for her that night, so Millward went with the next person who she came across. That man happened to be Peter Sutcliffe.

Sutcliffe drove Millward around three miles near to the Manchester Royal Infirmary and found a suitable spot in a car park which was regularly used by prostitutes and their clients. Sutcliffe wasted little time with Millward, and attacked her the second she exited his car. Millward put up resistance at first, but was unable to overpower Sutcliffe. After several more blows to the head, Millward slipped into unconsciousness. Sutcliffe dragged her to a nearby fence and slashed her stomach so badly that her intestines had spilled from her insides. Her body was discovered the following morning.

Ann Rooney (Survived)

Very little is known about Sutcliffe's next alleged victim. 22-year old Ann Rooney was attacked in Horsforth, Leeds almost 10 months after Vera Millward's murder.

Ann Rooney was not a prostitute. She was attacked by an unknown assailant on March 2nd, 1979 by several blows to the head from behind. Not much else is known, and Ann Rooney may not even be a Ripper victim at all. While she was attacked from behind in the same manner as all other Ripper victims, the hammer blows seem to come from one smaller than the Ripper regularly used, shedding doubt on her attacker's identity.

There are rumors that Sutcliffe confessed to being her attacker in private although no official documents exist to confirm this. The closest written confirmation of this is a British documentary from 1996 called "Silent Victims: The Untold Story of the Yorkshire Ripper". The documentary states that Sutcliffe confessed to a 1979 attack around

Leeds College, although minor details differ from other sources.

Josephine Whitaker

"Following Millward, the compulsion inside me seemed to lay dormant, but eventually the feeling came welling up, and each time they were more random and indiscriminate. I now realized I had the urge to kill any woman and I thought that this would eventually get me caught, but I think that in my sub-conscious this was what I really wanted."

This statement from Sutcliffe is a revealing insight into his state of mind during this period. The fact that Sutcliffe, by now, has admitted to himself that any woman is a target for his vengeance makes him even more dangerous. He is now no longer bound by a specific victim type; all women are potential targets.

It may not be coincidence then, that the Yorkshire Ripper's next six victims were all 'innocent' victims. None of them had links to the sex trade in any way.

On April 4th 1979, Sutcliffe had been out drinking with his friend Trevor Birdsall. After dropping him home, Sutcliffe turned around and headed into Halifax for his next victim. As he passed by the fields of Savile Park, he noticed 19-year-old clerical worker Josephine Whitaker walking through the field alone.

Due to Whitaker not being a prostitute, Sutcliffe would need to drastically change his modus operandi in order to get close to her. It was very unlikely that a non-prostitute would accept a car ride with a stranger; so instead, Sutcliffe parked his car, concealed his hammer and screwdriver in his coat, and simply caught up with Whitaker as she walked.

They walked for several minutes before Sutcliffe stopped and pretending he was looking a distant clock tower for the time. In actuality, he was unsheathing his hammer ready to attack Whitaker from behind. He floored her with one brutal blow to her head, then dragged her into a bush away from the nearby main road. Sutcliffe exposed her body, at which point Whitaker was loudly screaming in pain. Sutcliffe then viciously mutilated her body with a screwdriver, stabbing her total of twenty-seven times across her stomach, back and legs. He even used the screwdriver to penetrate her vagina; an act of final humiliation.

This brutality marked an escalation in Sutcliffe's tactics. Firstly, he willingly engaged in conversation with his victim without the safety of his vehicle to flee in case of problems. Secondly, the mutilation of the vagina suggests Sutcliffe had recently suffered bouts of sexual inadequacy. While reports from his wife never state this, it is common for serial killers to substitute genitalia for blunt objects when they are unable to successfully perform sexual acts or commit rape. Additionally, there was bite marks discovered on Josephine Whitaker's left breast, although Sutcliffe denied he did this.

Barbara Leach

It would be 150 days after the murder of Josephine Whitaker that the Ripper would claim his next victim.

On the evening of September 1st 1979, 20-year-old psychology student Barbara Leach had been drinking with friends the Manville Arms in Great Horton, Bradford. In the early hours of the next morning, Leach and her friends left the pub, with Leach dispersing from the group to make her way home.

Unbeknownst to Leach, Sutcliffe had been watching her group from afar. When he noticed Leach become isolated, he drove ahead of her and stopped his car. He waited for Leach to pass him by before making his attack. He assaulted Leach from behind in a dark alleyway in Ash Grove with a hammer blow to the head. Once subdued, Sutcliffe dragged leach into a nearby grassy area before undressing her. Once her breasts and genitals were exposed, Sutcliffe stabbed her repeatedly with the same screwdriver he had used to end the life of Josephine Whitaker five months previous.

He hid Leach's body behind some nearby dustbins, covering them with pieces of junk, rubble and soil. Her body was discovered the following day by police after Leach's roommates had reported her missing. The police had no doubts that Leach had been a victim of the Yorkshire Ripper, but even more concerning was that the Ripper's two most recent victims were not related to the prostitution trade. If his potential victim pool expanded, it would make his actions more difficult to predict.

Sutcliffe claims that at this point, his compulsion to kill was "totally out of his control".

Marguerite Walls

Peter Sutcliffe's cooling-off period between murders was already sporadic and unpredictable. Sometimes he would go only weeks between kills, while other times he would wait significantly longer. After Barbara Leach, Sutcliffe would not strike again for almost a year.

As with his previous two victims, Marguerite Walls was not related to the sex trade in any way. She was a 47-year-old civil servant for the Department of Science and Education in Pudsey, Leeds. On 20th August 1980, Walls left her office around 10pm after working late. She made her way towards her home in Farsley, unaware that Peter Sutcliffe was following her.

Sutcliffe parked up his vehicle and proceeded to follow Walls on foot. As they reached an isolated residential area, Sutcliffe blitz attacked Walls from behind with a hammer blow to the head. As she fell to the ground, he attacked her further while referring to her as a "filthy prostitute", despite her not being. Then, in a strange change of modus operandi, Sutcliffe tied a rope around Walls' neck. He used it to drag her from the area of attack into a nearby garden which was sufficiently hidden enough to carry out her murder. He then used the rope he had tied around her neck to strangle her, a noticeable change in his method of killing.

Sutcliffe left her body in the residential garden. He covered Walls' body with leaves, grass and soil so that he could prolong the process of discovering her. She was found the following day by two gardeners.

Peter Sutcliffe's deviation of his usual signature marks a noticeable escalation point in his crimes. Sutcliffe would later declare that he knowingly adapted his methods of murder due to the stigma of the word "Ripper" surrounding him. Despite this, Sutcliffe found that "strangulation was even more horrible and took longer." Successfully, this change served to lead the Yorkshire Police down a wrong path, initially believing that the murder of Margeurite Walls was entirely unrelated to the Yorkshire Ripper.

Upadya Bandara (Survived)

Sutcliffe attacked 34-year-old Upadya Bandara in Leeds on the night of September 24th 1980, only 35 days after the murder of Marguerite Walls.

Whilst walking home from a friend's house at around 10:30pm, Bandara was attacked by Sutcliffe in his usual signature manner. As with his previous victim, Sutcliffe tried to strangle Bandara with a length of rope around her neck. As he dragged her to an ideal location to murder her, Bandara's pleas for help were heard by nearby neighbors. Fearing for his discovery, Sutcliffe fled the scene, leaving Bandara alive.

Due to the lack of usual signatures (no stab wounds, no exposing of the body, Bandara was not a prostitute), Bandara's attack was not immediately thought to be the work of the Ripper, and given that her wounds mirrored those of Marguerite Walls, the police initially thought a new killer was on the loose.

Theresa Sykes (Survived)

By late 1980, Sutcliffe was now an unstoppable killing machine. He no longer desired contact with the women he murdered, and was as unpredictable as ever in both his cooling-off periods and victim choice.

On November 5th 1980 at around 8pm, Sutcliffe carried out yet another impulsive blitz attack on a girl named Theresa Sykes, only 16 years of age. Again in Huddersfield, Sykes was returning from a nearby grocery store and was only a few yards away from her home. Sutcliffe caught up with her and dealt a hammer blow to the back of her head, immediately knocking her to the ground.

Sutcliffe dealt another blow to her as she lay on the floor, but her screams alerted the attention of her neighbors and Sykes' boyfriend, who chased after Sutcliffe as he ran away. Sutcliffe hid in a nearby grassy area until he considered it safe to leave. This was the closest Sutcliffe ever came to being captured in the act.

This attack was also a deviation from Sutcliffe's usual methods. It was the earliest he had ever attacked one of his victims (which would later assist in his downfall), and he carried out the assault in a largely residential area.

Jacqueline Hill

The night of November 17th 1980 would see the Yorkshire Ripper's reign of terror come to an end. On a bleak winter evening, 20-year-old student Jacqueline Hill was walking home from an educational seminar when she was spotted by Sutcliffe.

Sutcliffe's previous attack had been less than two weeks ago, although he hadn't succeeded in murdering his victim which was perhaps the reason for his short downtime. Sutcliffe was sitting in his vehicle outside the Arndale Shopping Centre in Leeds when he first noticed Hill, and slowly followed her until he was able to stop in front of her.

He silently followed her on foot for a short distance before striking her from behind with a hammer. Almost immediately, another woman came walking towards both Sutcliffe and Hill, to which Sutcliffe quickly pulled Hill onto a desolate area of land behind the shopping center.

When the passer-by had vanished from sight, Sutcliffe lay Hill on the floor and murdered her by stabbing her with his screwdriver in the torso and eye. Her body was discovered the following day.

Part 2: Interviews

Over the course of the Ripper investigation, Peter Sutcliffe was interviewed by police a total of nine times. For every single one, Sutcliffe had an alibi and was able to convince police that he was unable to have committed the crimes he was being questioned about.

Sutcliffe's manipulation aside, it should also be noted that West Yorkshire Police did not handle their interview process with the rigid attention it required. Due to lack of reports and official documentation being kept, many times Sutcliffe was questioned; police thought it was their first time interviewing him. Due to the heavy reliance on the hoax letters and audio tape sent by John Humble,

Sutcliffe was able to avoid most questions with ease. In many cases, enough time had passed between the event and the date of questioning that the alibis he offered were casually backed up by his friends, family and wife without much hesitation on their part.

Interview #1 – November 2nd 1977

Sutcliffe's first interview by police was due the now infamous £5 note incident. The serial number on the note was traced back to Sutcliffe's company, T&WH Holdings Ltd, who had issued the note to one of 8000 employees.

Sutcliffe's alibi for the night of the murder of Jean Jordan was that he had been at home all night and retired to bed at around 11:30pm.

Regarding the second visit to Jean Jordan's body, Sutcliffe's air-tight alibi was that he had been at a housewarming party, which was indeed true. Both events were confirmed by Sutcliffe's wife.

Interview #2 – November 8th 1977

Only six days later, Sutcliffe was again interviewed regarding the £5 note incident, albeit by different police officers. He gave the same stories as previously, again confirmed by his wife. In addition, Sutcliffe's mother also confirmed that she had been with Peter on the same night and that he had driven her home after their party.

Interview #3 – August 13th 1978

Sutcliffe's license plate on his red Ford Corsair had been noticed several times in Bradford's red-light district. When questioned, Sutcliffe claimed that he had driven through the area for work purposes, and that he had never used a prostitute in his life. Sonia backed up her husband's statements by saying that he rarely left the house in the evening and that the pair was out on the night of the Vera Millward's murder.

Interview #4 – November 23rd 1978

Police would interview Sutcliffe again regarding his vehicles. He had recently purchased a Sunbeam Rapier and sold his Ford Corsair. Police would check his tyres to see if they matched any of the prints found at crime scenes, but luckily Sutcliffe had recently replaced them all with brand new ones.

Interview #5 – July 29 1979

This would be Sutcliffe's most intense interview of all. His black Sunbeam Rapier had been spotted a total of 36 times by surveillance teams in Bradford, Leeds and Manchester. This would be the only time in which police seriously considered him as a suspect, as one of the investigating officers noted that there "something not quite right" about Peter Sutcliffe. Luckily for him, police were unaware that this was his fifth time being interviewed. The officers at the time assumed this to be Sutcliffe's first questioning.

As with his previous interviews, Sutcliffe claimed that his reasons for regularly passing through the red-light areas were work related. Again, these claims were backed up by Sonia. One of the investigators realized during this interview that Sutcliffe matched almost every known detail they had regarding the offender: he fit the physical description, he was regularly seen at the crime scene locations, he was a lorry driver, and he had a slight gap between two of his teeth – something which Marilyn Moore ascertained after her assault. The same officer later discovered that Sutcliffe could also have been the receiver of the £5 note from T&WH Holdings Ltd.

Unfortunately, by the time it came for senior detectives to look into their colleagues' suspicions, the West Yorkshire Police had become reliant on the hoax letters and audio tape, allowing Sutcliffe to evade capture once again.

Interview #6 – October 23rd 1979

Sutcliffe was again interviewed regarding the frequency of his licence plate being spotted in multiple red light districts. Unfortunately, the investigating officer in this case was unaware of the Sutcliffe's previous interview which raised suspicions in other police officers. However, after taking samples of Sutcliffe's handwriting, he was unsurprisingly eliminated as a suspect due to it not being a match with the handwriting of the hoax letter.

Interview #7 – January 13th 1980

A third interview regarding the owner of the £5 note brought the police to Sutcliffe's house once more. By this point, the possible owners of the £5 note had been reduced down a pool of only 241 people (one of which was Peter Sutcliffe).

Sutcliffe was also questioned regarding his whereabouts on the night of the murder of Barbara Leach; however he was unable to offer one. Sutcliffe's house and car were also examined by officers, but nothing was discovered.

Due to errors made by West Yorkshire Police, there were no records of Sutcliffe's previous interviews, meaning officers could not match up the rousing suspicions from other officers. The interest in Sutcliffe then fell by the wayside.

Interview #8 – January 30th 1980

A further interview regarding Sutcliffe's frequent passes through red-light areas took place in Leeds while Sutcliffe loaded his lorry for a delivery. He also invented an alibi for the night of the murder of Barbara Leach, which he told officers his wife would confirm.

Throughout this interview, Sutcliffe was wearing the boots which he had worn during the murder of Josephine Whitaker. Boots which the officers in front of him had a picture of as prints from them were discovered at the Whitaker crime scene. Luckily for Sutcliffe, officers did not enquire.

Interview #9 – February 1980

A senior officer was unhappy with a previous report filed by one of his colleagues which detailed Sutcliffe's vehicle sightings and alibis. A re-investigation was ordered, but Sutcliffe was able to provide alibis for his car sightings, all of which his wife would confirm.

Part 3: Arrest, Confession & Trial

Arrest

On 2nd January 1981, Peter Sutcliffe visited Sheffield with the intentions of murdering his next victim. At 4pm that afternoon, he left his house for the final time.

24-year-old prostitute Olivia Reivers was spotted by Sutcliffe around 9pm. The pair negotiated a price for Reivers' services and settled on £10. Reivers claimed she knew an ideal location for them to perform the deed, and directed Sutcliffe to an isolated car park of a multi-national office headquarters.

It is unknown if Sutcliffe had planned on going through with the act of sex with Reivers, but regardless, he was unable to become sufficiently aroused. He therefore struggled to find a reason to request Reivers exit his car so that they could make love on the ground. While they pair chatted, two police officers were doing a routine patrol when the spotted Sutcliffe's vehicle parked up.

The officers approached Sutcliffe and Reivers and questioned their intentions, despite it being quite obvious. Sutcliffe told them his name was Peter Williams and that Reivers was his girlfriend. In perhaps the luckiest moment of the entire case (for both the police and Reivers), one of the officers recognized Olivia Reivers' face. He knew that she was actually a working girl who regularly slept with men in this area.

The officers told Reivers to get in her police car. Sutcliffe then asked if he could relieve himself up a nearby oil storage tank. They allowed him to, to which Sutcliffe did while subtly disposing of his intended murder weapons which he had concealed on his person throughout his interactions with Reivers. They made a small clink as he lowered them to the ground which Sutcliffe prayed that the officers hadn't heard. As he returned, the officers ran a check on Sutcliffe's vehicle license plate. In another stroke of luck, it turned out they were fake, giving the officers enough cause to arrest Sutcliffe.

Peter soon confessed that he had lied about his name, his reasons being that he didn't want his wife to find out he was being unfaithful. It should be noted that during this whole incident, the arresting officers did not have the slightest idea that the man they were apprehending was the Yorkshire Ripper. They took Sutcliffe to the police station where he remained until the next morning. Sutcliffe's was called to be told that her husband would not be coming home that evening.

The following day, Sutcliffe was transferred to Dewsbury police station. He was initially questioned by officers regarding the fake license plates on his vehicle, but eventually his presence was noticed by several members of the Ripper Task Force. They noted that he possessed many of the characteristics of the perpetrator they were chasing; dark hair, bushy beard, gap in his teeth, lorry driver, Yorkshire local, size 7-8 shoe, B-type blood group. Several senior officers were notified to the fact that they may have the Yorkshire Ripper in custody.

Confession

The officer who initially apprehended Sutcliffe remained calm, and would then make perhaps the most inquisitive decision throughout the whole case. He remembered that Sutcliffe had requested to urinate during his questioning and, despite Sutcliffe's prayers, had heard a vague clinking sound as he did. He returned to the area where he first approached Sutcliffe and checked around the storage tank where Sutcliffe had relieved himself. He discovered Peters Sutcliffe's murder weapons lying on a nearby wall; his ball-peen hammer and a knife. He was now ninety-nine percent sure they had the Yorkshire Ripper in custody.

A search of Sutcliffe's house was quickly authorized. The police discovered a large collection of ball-peen hammers, many of which had previously been used as murder weapons. Over the next forty-eight hours, officers scrambled to gather as much information regarding Sutcliffe's whereabouts during the time of every murder as they could, all while Sutcliffe was questioned by detectives. Sutcliffe remained calm throughout, rationally answering every question posed to him. It was not until early afternoon on Sunday 4th January that he began to show signs of distress.

At 2:40pm the same day, Peter Sutcliffe was told that a hammer and knife belonging to him were found at the spot he was arrested. Sutcliffe did not put up any more restraint. He then calmly announced to the interviewing detective that he was the Yorkshire Ripper.

Sutcliffe showed little emotion during his ensuing confession. He calmly described all of his attacks, recalling even the most minor of details. It seemed on the surface that Sutcliffe was relieved to have finally been caught. He was not aggressive or uncooperative at any point during his entire confession. He only had one request; for him to be the one to inform his wife Sonia of who he really was.

Trial

On May 5th 1981, Peter Sutcliffe pleaded not guilty to thirteen accounts of murder, but guilty to manslaughter. After giving his reasons for killing, which Sutcliffe claimed were "voices from God", a jury deliberated whether or not Sutcliffe's state of mind excused him from his actions. On May 22nd 1981, a majority verdict found him guilty of thirteen accounts of murder, seven accounts of attempted murder, and declared him sane. He was sentenced to twenty separate life sentences to be served in succession.

Part 4: Letters & Audio Tape

Over the course of the Yorkshire Ripper investigation, police received hundreds of letters and documents detailing advice and information regarding the supposed identity of the perpetrator. The majority of the letters were well-received and served to aid the police's investigation, however, as with many high profile cases, a number of hoaxes were received which led the police down a wrong path.

The official stance is that Peter Sutcliffe himself did not contact the press or police regarding his crimes in any way. The only involvement he had in such matters was that he was interviewed by police on a number of occasions and enjoyed reading about his attacks in local newspapers. He did not consciously inject himself into the investigation at all.

Between March 1978 and March 1979, West Yorkshire Police were sent three letters which they believed to be from the actual killer.

8th March 1978

[Transcription of the letter]:

"Dear Sir

I am sorry I cannot give my name for obvious reasons. I am the Ripper. I've been dubbed a maniac by the Press but not by you, you call me clever and I am. You and your mates haven't a clue that photo in the paper gave me fits and that bit about killing myself, no chance. I've got things to do; my purpose to rid the streets of them sluts. My one regret is that young lassie McDonald, did not know cause changed routine that night. Up to number 8 now you say 7 but remember Preston '75. Get about you know. You were right I travel a bit. You probably look for me in Sunderland, don't bother, I am not daft, just posted letter there on one of my trips. Not a bad place compared with Chapeltown and Manningham and other places. Warn whores to keep off streets because I feel it coming on again.

Sorry about young lassie.

Yours respectfully

Jack the Ripper

Might write again later I not sure last one really deserve it. Whores getting younger each time. Old slut next time I hope. Huddersfield never again, too small close call last one."

On the surface, this letter could appear to genuinely be from the killer himself. The "Preston 75" which the author makes reference to was the murder of a woman named Joan Harrison who was longed considered to be a Ripper victim but was confirmed not to be in 2011. While the bizarre signing off of "Jack the Ripper" seems detrimental to the author taking credit for the Yorkshire Ripper murders, it was possibly an attempt by the actual author to make it an obvious hoax.

14th March 1978

The second later came one week later, presumed by the police to be the same author.

[Transcription of the letter]:

"Dear Sir.

I have already written Chief constable, Oldfield "a man I respect" concerning the recent Ripper murders. I told him and I am telling you to warn those whores I'll strike and soon when heat cools off. About the

Mcdonald lassie I did not know that she was decent and I am sorry I changed my routine that night, Up to number 8 now you say 7 but remember Preston 75. Easy picking them up don't even have to try, you think they're learn but they don't Most are young lassies, next time try older one I hope. Police haven't a clue yet and I don't leave any I am very clever and don't think of looking for any fingerprints cause there aren't any and don't look for me up in Sunderland cause I not stupid just passed through the place not a bad place compared with Chapeltown and Manningham can't walk the streets for them whore, Don't forget warn them I feel it coming on again if I get the chance, Sorry about lassie I didn't know

Yours respectfully

Jack the Ripper

Might write again after another ones' gone
Maybe Liverpool or even Manchester again,
to hot here in Yorkshire, Bye.

I have given advance warning so it's yours
and theirs fault."

The "MacDonald lassie" the author refers to
is Jayne MacDonald, the Ripper's fifth
victim. She was only 16 years old and wasn't
a sex worker, which is what the author
means by "decent".

The writing style and language matched the
first letter, as well as both letters making
references to "Chapeltown and

Manningham", concluding that they were both written by the same culprit.

March 23rd 1979

[Transcription of the letter]:

"Dear Officer. March 23rd 79

Sorry I haven't written, about a year to be exact, but I haven't been up North for quite a while. I wasn't kidding last time I wrote saying the whore would be older this time and maybe I'd strike in Manchester for a change. You should have taken heed. That bit about her being in hospital, funny the lady mentioned something about being in the same hospital before I stopped her whoring ways. The lady won't worry about hospitals now will she I bet you are wondering how come I haven't been to work for ages, well I would have been if it hadn't been for your curserred coppers I had the lady just where I wanted her and was about to strike when one of your cursen police cars stopped right outside the lane, he must have been a dumb copper cause he didn't say anything, he didn't know how close he was to catching me. Tell you the truth I thought I was collared, the lady said do not worry about the coppers, little did she know that bloody copper saved her neck. That was last month, so I don't know when I will get back on the job but I know it won't be Chapeltown too bloody hot there maybe Bradfords Manningham. Might write again if up North.

Jack the Ripper

P S Did you get letter I sent to Daily Mirror in Manchester."

Despite the many references to small details of the Ripper's crimes throughout all three letters, the author did not include any information which wasn't already known to the public. In many cases, a serial killer will include details which only he and the police are aware of in order to confirm his identity. It seems that the author of these three letters tried to do such a thing multiple times ("Preston 75", the story regarding the "coppers" being nearby during one of his murders) but was unable to provide any solid proof of who he was.

Additionally, the language portrayed in each letter suggests someone literate enough to express himself, but not someone educated to a high level by any means. The constant grammar errors, spelling mistakes, misuse of quotation marks and general disarray of the language points to happened to fit the profile of the Yorkshire Ripper exactly: disorganized in his methods, but self-aware enough to understand how to evade capture.

Wearside Jack: The Audio Tape

On 17th June 1979, police received an audio tape from someone claiming to be the Yorkshire Ripper. They immediately thought they had a break in the case. The transcription of the audio tape is as follows:

"I'm Jack. I see you are still having no luck catching me. I have the greatest respect for you George, but Lord! You are no nearer catching me now than four years ago when I started. I reckon your boys are letting you down, George. They can't be much good, can they?"

The "George" in question was Assistant Chief Constable George Oldfield who was overseeing the Ripper investigation, and again, his involvement with the case was widely publicized. The tape was initially considered genuine by West Yorkshire Police, and so turned their attention to the Sunderland area of England to hunt for the killer as the voice on the tape spoke with a heavy Wearside accent. He had also several speech defects: a minor stammer and a distinctive pronunciation of the letter's'. Several voice experts thought it would be quite simple to locate the person based on his voice characteristics quite easily. However, the assumption that the voice on the tape was the real killer would be the biggest mistake the police would make.

Around 40,000 men from the Sunderland area were questioned – but of course, nothing would come of it – as the real killer lived in Bradford. This tape came just before the murder of Barbara Leach in September 1979, and because of the contents of the tape, caused the police to focus their investigation in entirely the wrong direction. While the police were investigating people in the Sunderland region, three more women would die at the hands of the Yorkshire Ripper.

The identity of the author of the letters and the voice on the audio tape would remain a mystery until long after Sutcliffe's arrest. After Sutcliff's capture, he denied all accusations of being the culprit behind any sort of police contact, and authorities had no reason to doubt him, especially as Sutcliffe's voice would not match the voice on the tape. This realization was a heavy blow to the West Yorkshire Police. By believing that the tape was real, they were led astray and in turn, helped Sutcliffe to evade capture by ruling him out based on voice and handwriting samples.

It was not until 2005, 25 years after Sutcliffe was caught, that the identity of the hoaxer was revealed. A small piece of evidence relating to one of the letters was discovered in a forensic laboratory the same year which held vital DNA clues to the identity of the writer. As DNA had advanced to levels far beyond what was capable in 1981, it didn't take long for investigators to match the sample they had taken to a man named John Humble; a Sunderland-based unemployed alcoholic.

Humble admitted to being the perpetrator behind all of the hoax items. His voice also matched the recorded voice. He was arrested for perverting the course of justice, although Humble claims that this wasn't his intentions. He stated that he simply desired fame and notoriety, and admitted that he felt shame and embarrassment over his actions. He was imprisoned in 2006, but has subsequently been released and now lives a free man as of 2013.

Part 5: Psychological Profile

Peter Sutcliffe is what FBI serial killer classifications would label as disorganized. What this means is that Sutcliffe's crimes were impulsive, reckless and largely unplanned. Many times, he would simply leave his house with the intention to kill; nothing else. His victims were women he had never seen before. He did not stalk them for days and learn their routines in order to strike at the perfect moment. Instead, he acted at a moment's notice.

Sutcliffe's method of murder is what would become his signature. A signature is a particular act performed by the killer which he or she is compelled to leave as, without it, their needs are not fulfilled. Signatures are usually what investigators will use in order to link crimes of a single perpetrator together. In the case of Peter Sutcliffe, it could be considered that his blitz hammer attacks from behind would be his signature, but this would be inaccurate. This was simply Sutcliffe's way of gaining control over this victim. Again, another factor which contributes to Sutcliffe's categorization of a disorganized offender.

Sutcliffe's signature, then, would be his stabbing of the victim's torso with his screwdriver. This was the part Sutcliffe needed. In many cases when Sutcliffe was unable to act out this particular part of his fantasy, he would strike again a lot sooner than if he had been able to fulfil his desires. In the cases where screwdriver insertion was not apparent, police initially failed to link these crimes to the Yorkshire Ripper.

The fact that Sutcliffe was compelled to stab the torsos of his victims would be indicative of his motivation to kill women in the first place. There are multiple theories abound as to why the Yorkshire Ripper did what he did, the most common one being that Peter Sutcliffe simply hated prostitutes.

A story from Peter's childhood regarding his first experiences of sex workers were likely a crucial factor in his suppressed hatred of them. As a child (exact dates are unknown), Peter's father John Sutcliffe had discovered that his wife, Kathleen, had arranged a night in a hotel with a secret lover behind John's back. When John found out about her plans, he dragged along Peter to confront her in her hotel room. It was all true. John and Peter Sutcliffe discovered Kathleen Sutcliffe at the hotel waiting her arrival of her secret boyfriend. John proceeded to humiliate Kathleen in front of Peter, referring to her as a 'whore', 'prostitute' and 'slut'.

From this point on, Peter Sutcliffe's perception of women offering their services to strange men may have become a twisted notion to him. In his mind, he would associate the act with deceit, heartbreak and grief. Finally, when he was the victim of minor robbery and humiliation at the hands of the very first prostitute he tried to elicit the services of (whether this was for sexual gratification or to appease his murderous impulses is unknown), this tipped him over the edge.

Sutcliffe's "voices from God" which he claimed during his trial (and in his subsequent confessions) were his primary motivation for the murders are still a subject of debate. Indeed, during his employment as a gravedigger, it was reported that Sutcliffe's behavior became bizarre and outlandish. He would occasionally lie in freshly-dug graves pretending to be a corpse, and then leap out at his colleagues when they passed by. He claimed that the voices spoke to him as he stood in the grave of Polish man Bronisław Zapolski, although no further elaboration was made. Sutcliffe would later say that he "was on a divine mission from God" to rid the world of prostitutes.

[Author's note: it should be mentioned that I once had personal contact with Peter Sutcliffe in 2011 in a communal area of Broadmoor Hospital. We did not speak of his crimes, although I overheard him make an off-key remark that 'the voices' were telling him to 'get a cup of tea', suggesting he no longer (or perhaps, never did) take such claims seriously even himself. Also, I once had contact with Peter's brother, Carl Sutcliffe who showed me a letter which Peter had sent to him. A particular line regarding 'religion being a deus ex machina for those who want early parole' stood out to me.]

A further theory addresses the infertility issues Peter and Sonia battled. Despite Sutcliffe's horrific crimes, he and his wife maintained a largely happy marriage (until she became aware of what he had done). The realization that a happy couple would be unable to have children is a devastating discovery for anyone, let alone for someone who had such a twisted perception of the world as Sutcliffe. Not long after being told this news, Sutcliffe would carry out his first attack, and throughout his spree, would focus his mutilations on areas of the stomach and torso of his victims, which possibly indicated a subconscious desire to prevent others from reproducing. He was projecting his own suffering onto others in the only way he knew how.

Whichever theory is accurate, it should be remembered that Peter Sutcliffe's motivation could likely be a combination of factors. The complexities of human mentality are made up of conscious and unconscious desires, many of which are beyond our capacity to access. Additionally, given Peter Sutcliffe's childhood traumas, skewed perception of sex and relationships and a primal desire to kill, a perfect storm was created which manifested as homicidal violence.

Part 6: Imprisonment & Current Status

Since his incarceration in 1981, Sutcliffe chose to be known as Peter William Coonan, his mother's maiden name, in an effort to protect his notoriety and his family who still retained the name Sutcliffe (although by this point, the name Sutcliffe was already synonymous with the Ripper murders).

Sutcliffe remained at HMP Parkhurst, his first prison, for three years. Whilst there, he was seriously injured by a fellow inmate with a broken coffee car which caused Sutcliffe to require stiches in his face.

In 1984, Sutcliffe was diagnosed with paranoid schizophrenia by prison psychiatrists and in turn was sent to Broadmoor Hospital where he would remain for over thirty years. Sutcliffe has been the target of multiple violent attacks due to his status as one of the Britain's most infamous murderers. In 1996, Sutcliffe was strangled in his room by another inmate, but was quickly rescued by nearby staff. In 1997, he was famously attacked with a pen that caused Sutcliffe to lose vision on his left side. In 2007, he was attacked again by an inmate who tried to stab him with a cutlery knife while screaming that he was going to "blind him in his other eye".

In 2010, Sutcliffe launched an appeal requesting a minimum term for his crimes to be set, offering possibility of parole after an agreed date if his mental state allowed. After the courts took into account his psychological state and the severity of his crimes, it was officially decided that Peter Sutcliffe will spend the rest of his life in prison.

In 2015, Sutcliffe was officially declared "no longer mentally ill" by psychiatrists. He was medically cleared of requiring treatment from a mental hospital and was declared fit to return to prison. He was transferred to Frankland Prison, Durham in August 2016, where he will likely live out the remainder of his days.

Conclusion

Not since the crimes of Jack the Ripper in 1888 has a British murderer made such a lasting impact on the world. The Yorkshire Ripper holds one of the highest body counts in recent memory; 13 murders and a string of other attacks which would later yield additional deaths and tragedy. The frequency at which Peter Sutcliffe mercilessly took lives is something which few modern serial killers will ever surpass.

What makes Peter Sutcliffe a figure of terror is the fact that he is simply a working class everyman, but one who harbored a violent compulsion he was unable to control. The fact that the Yorkshire Ripper evaded capture for six years, despite being at the forefront of investigations, is a testament to his ability to hide in plain sight. It is Peter Sutcliffe's banality which adds an additional layer of fear to an already terrifying character.

To suggest that anything positive could come of Sutcliffe's horrific crimes is absurd and would be insulting to anyone affected by his actions, however, with great tragedy often comes severe wake-up calls. In this case, the West Yorkshire Police learnt harsh lessons regarding their incompetence and inability to act to the required standard. Because of simple errors which were caused by the police's carelessness, Peter Sutcliffe evaded capture for longer than was necessary, resulting in additional lives lost.

How much responsibility of the Ripper's crimes lies in the hands of West Yorkshire Police is open for debate, but it should be remembered that, at the time, the police were ill-equipped to handle an investigation of this magnitude. It was unheard of for such a reign of terror to be carried out on such a large scale.

Since the Ripper's crimes over thirty-five years ago, forensic science and criminal profiling has come a significantly long way. There have been very few instances of serial killers claiming any more than a handful of victims before being captured, and certainly no victims carrying out murder sprees on the same scale as Peter Sutcliffe's. Hopefully, the crimes of the Yorkshire Ripper have taught police to be prepared for atrocities which are beyond comprehension.

Fred & Rose West

The Couple Who Killed Shocking True Serial Killers Stories

Roger Harrington

Introduction

Some of Britain's most horrific crimes took place in a seemingly normal home. Fred and Rosemary West lived with their nine children at 25 Cromwell Street, in Gloucester, England. The large family was tightknit and was fairly well-liked in the community, but the West household was far from a normal, wholesome home.

Fred and Rose used their house as equal parts brothel and torture dungeon. They put their children, lodgers, and strangers through horrific abuse, torture, and even murder. They did unspeakable things behind closed doors that would eventually give their house the nickname The Gloucester House of Horrors.

The story of Fred and Rose West is proof that we never really know what is going on in other people's lives, and that evil can be happening in the most mundane places, right under our noses.

Early Lives

Frederick Walter Stephen West was born on September 29th, 1941 to Walter Stephen West, and Daisy Hannah Hill, in Much Marcle, Herefordshire. He was their first surviving child, of what would eventually be six children: John, David, Daisy, Douglas, Kathleen, and Gwen. The Wests were an extremely poor farming family who lived in a run-down house without electricity or running water.

Fred alleged that he and his siblings were subject to sexual abuse from both parents. Walter would routinely rape his daughters, and Fred was introduced to sex by his mother at age 12. Fred also claims his father taught him about bestiality at a very young age. The pair would have sexual intercourse with the farm's sheep. Walter West told his son to, "Do what you want, just don't get caught doing it."

Fred's brother, Doug, claims none of Fred's allegations of abuse are true. However, later crimes committed by Fred and his brother John are certainly in keeping with people who have suffered an abusive childhood.

Fred was not a good student. He never fully grasped reading and writing, and was largely illiterate for the rest of his life. Fred was also bullied by his classmates. His mother, Daisy, would often go to the school and yell at teachers for getting Fred in trouble, or at other students for bullying her son. Fred ended up leaving school at 15.

When he was 17, Fred was in a terrible motorcycle accident, and joined the long line of eventual serial killers who sustained a significant head injury in their early life. He was driving his Lambretta down a local street, and collided with a woman going the opposite direction.

Fred broke an arm and a leg, fractured his skull, and was in a coma for eight days. He damaged his frontal cortex; the part of the brain in charge of sexual behavior, judgement, and emotional expression. After this accident, his family noticed he lost control of his emotions, and became even more sexually aggressive than he had been before.

At 19, Fred sustained another head injury. He was at a local youth club, when he began assaulting a young woman. She fought back and ended up pushing Fred off the fire escape. He was unconscious for 24 hours.

In 1961 Fred's attitude continued to decline. He was arrested and fined for theft after stealing a watch strap and a cigarette case.

Fred continued the West family pattern of abuse. He and his brothers followed their father's example, and would also rape his sisters. In 1961, Fred alleges he got his 13 year old sister, Katherine, who they called Kitty, pregnant. His mother reported him to the police. He was arrested, and disowned by his family. It has been speculated that because of his mother's own sexual relationship with her son, Daisy West was jealous of her Fred's relationship with his sister, and only called the police to punish him.

On November 9th, 1961, Fred was charged with assault against a minor for his attacks on his sister. However, when the trial came around, Kitty refused to give evidence against her brother. The case collapsed.

It is not known what happened to the child the two siblings conceived, or indeed whether it ever existed. Fred was known for being a compulsive liar and though there is little doubt he subjected his sister to sexual abuse, he may not have actually conceived with her. Fred also later claimed to several people that he was able to perform crude home abortions. Perhaps he began practicing this skill with his sister.

Fred went to live with an aunt for a short period of time, but eventually was allowed back into the West's house. He began dating an ex-girlfriend, Catherine "Rena" Costello. Rena was a sex worker who was pregnant with another man's child at the time. On November 17th, 1962, she married Fred West, and the couple moved to Lancashire.

Anne Marie, the couple's first biological daughter said of Rena, "My rebellious mother was obsessed with my father and wildly attracted to his strange gypsy looks and bushy brown hair. She wanted him and that was that."

On February 22nd, 1963, Rena's daughter, Charmaine, was born. Charmaine was mixed race and was, therefore, obviously not Fred's child. The couple told Rena's family that she had miscarried the child she was carrying before she married Fred, and that she and Fred had adopted Charmaine.

Soon after Charmaine's birth, Rena became pregnant again. On July 6th, 1964 Anne Marie was born.

The growing family moved to Scotland, where Fred allegedly became acquainted with James Gallogley, an elder in the church, and Alexander Gartshore. Gartshore, who was also the West's neighbor, confessed from prison that Fred had been a part of the paedophile ring the men ran.

In addition to his involvement in the sex ring, Fred may already have started his killing spree by this time. At least four young girls went missing while Fred and Rena were living in Glasgow; one of whom, by the name of Margaret McAvoy, Fred was known to have been acquainted with.

A former neighbor of the Wests said Fred had rented a garden plot adjacent to their houses. He was said to only work there very early in the morning, and he only grew plants on a small patch of it. The neighbor claimed Fred told him the rest of the plot was for "something special".

The garden plots were paved over in the 1970s as part of the M8 motorway expansion. Some believe that road holds secrets of further murders that Fred West took to his grave.

During his time in Scotland, Fred was working as an ice cream van driver. He was popular among the young people in the town, and it has been alleged he found several sexual assault victims through this job.

On November 4th, 1965, Fred West ran over and killed a four year old boy in his ice cream van. It is not known for certain whether this was deliberate. Fred was not prosecuted for this crime, but still decided to flee the area to avoid the scrutiny and hate of the locals. Fred, Rena, Charmaine, and Anne Marie, along with the children's nanny Isa McNeill, and a family friend Anna McFall,

all moved back to England. They lived in a caravan in Lakeside Caravan Park in Bishops Cleeve. Fred continued to be sexually aggressive with all three women, and physically abusive with the children.

Rena and Isa McNeill decided to move back to Scotland to escape Fred's abuse. They left the children with Fred and McFall, occasionally visiting, and attempting to get custody of the children. Fred refused to give them up.

Rena approached Constable Hazel Savage to tell her that Fred was a danger to the children. Savage took an interest in Fred from that point on, and kept the West family on her radar. She would later be instrumental in bringing Fred to justice.

Once settled in the caravan, Fred got a job in a slaughterhouse. It is believed that it was there that Fred West developed his obsession with dismembering corpses, and an interest in necrophilia. Nobody who knew him can remember Fred having such interests before this job.

Anna McFall had become infatuated with Fred during their time together, and the two began a relationship. Anna was consistently insistent that Fred get a legal divorce from Rena so the two could be together. Some suspect Fred got tired of her nagging.

In 1967, when Anna McFall was 8 months pregnant with Fred's child, she disappeared. Fred never reported her missing. Her remains wouldn't be found until 1994, when

Fred told the authorities where they might find her body.

Despite confessing to other killings, Fred never confessed to Anna's murder, and called her his one true love on more than one occasion, even after he married Rosemary. In 1994, Anna was found decapitated and dismembered in Fingerpost Field along with the fetus of her and Fred's unborn child. She was missing her fingers and toes.

A month after McFall's disappearance, Rena moved back in with Fred and her daughters. Fred forced Rena back into sex work in order to support the family. She did not wish to continue that life, and left again shortly after. Charmaine and Anne Marie were temporarily put into foster care.

In January 1968 Fred is strongly suspected to have committed another murder, though he has not been definitively tied to it. Fifteen-year-old Mary Bastholm went missing from a bus stop. Fred certainly had access to her. She was a waitress at Fred's local cafe, The Pop In, and Fred used to do construction work on the building behind the cafe.

On January 6th, 1968, Mary was on her way to Hardwicke to play a game of Monopoly with her boyfriend. She never showed up. A search of the area only turned up a few stray Monopoly pieces at a bridge near where Mary was waiting for the bus.

Years later, Fred confessed to his son, Stephen, that he had killed Mary, though he never admitted the murder to the police. Her body has still never been found.

On November 29th, 1968, 27-year-old Fred West met 15-year-old Rosemary Letts for the first time. He became immediately taken with her. She didn't feel the same way. Rose said of their first meeting, "I was waiting at the bus stop when I noticed this man looking at me. I didn't take to him at all. He was dirty and had work clothes on and looked quite old. This man started talking to me without asking my permission. Within a few minutes he had asked me out. He was like a tramp, a real; mess, and I said 'no'. I thought that was the end of that. Soon after our first meeting I saw him again at the bus stop. He got on the bus with me and started asking me out to pubs."

Fred brought a gift of a silk dress and a fur coat to Rose's workplace to ask her out. Considering the quality of the pieces, it is very likely Fred either stole the items, or got them from a previous murder victim, and gave them to Rose. Rose was impressed with his persistence, and agreed to go out with Fred.

Rosemary Pauline Letts was born on November 29th, 1953 in Devon, to William Andrew "Bill" Letts, and Daisy Gwendoline Fuller. She was the fifth of seven children.

Daisy had been given electro-convulsive shock therapy treatment for depression while she was pregnant with Rose. It is strongly suspected that Rose was born with brain damage because of this. She allegedly exhibited many signs of brain damage in her childhood.

Rose was a slow learner, would occasionally stare into space for extended periods of time, and would often sit alone and rock back and forth. She was also said to have a childlike demeanor, but be fairly sexually aggressive.

Bill ran the Letts household with military precision. There was a set schedule of chores for the children, and he would punish them with beatings if they did not adhere to it. If they did not get out of bed when he told them to, he would dump buckets of cold water over them. Bill would also often fly into fits of rage completely unprovoked. It has since been speculated that he was an undiagnosed, untreated schizophrenic.

Rose was subjected to much the same sexual abuse as Fred West. She was often beaten and raped by her father. Like Fred, Rose continued the cycle of abuse, and began sexually abusing her younger brothers.

As a teenager, Rose began working as a waitress at her sister's boyfriend's diner. She also began sex work in the parking lot of the diner. Rose was allegedly caught in bed with her sister's boyfriend, and was briefly kicked out of her house. When she moved back in just a few months later, rumors began in the neighborhood about a sexual relationship between Bill and Rose.

On her 15th birthday, Rose met Fred at a bus stop. Bill did not like the relationship between Fred and Rose and, as Rose was under the age of consent and Fred was more than 10 years her senior; he tried to get social services involved in their relationship.

At age 16 Rose moved out of her family home to go live with Fred in his trailer. She moved back and forth from the two residences, while Fred spent various stints in jail for theft during the first few months of their relationship.

Fred's children, Charmaine and Anne Marie, also moved between the trailer and foster care homes. While Fred was in jail, Rose was in charge of their care. She treated Fred's children horribly, beating them regularly. Anne Marie said, "It was obvious from the start that Rose had a hell of a temper, and was not able to control it".

Charmaine got the worst of Rose's abuse. Anne Marie said later stated that Charmaine, "would go out of her way to antagonize and aggravate our volatile stepmother", and that she "never missed a chance to remind rose about our real mother". It aggravated Rose even more that Charmaine would never cry when she was beaten.

Rose was kicked out of her family home for good when Bill found out she was pregnant. The family moved into a bigger home, a two-story house on Midland Road in Gloucester. On October 17th, 1970, Fred and Rose's first daughter, Heather, was born. Fred went back to jail for another theft charge on December 4th, 1970.

Midland Road

While he was in jail Rose's abuse of Fred's children got worse. In 1971 Rose wrote a suspicious note to Fred that read, "Darling, about Char. I think she liked to be handled rough. But darling, why do I have to be the one to do it. I would keep her for her own sake if it wasn't for the rest of the children. You can see Char coming out [i]n Anna now and I hate it."

In March of 1971 Charmaine was taken to the hospital with a puncture wound through her ankle. Doctors noted that the wound could have been from a knife, but they did not follow up on the potential abuse happening in the home, nor did they inform the police.

The family visited Fred in prison on June 17th, 1971. A few days later Charmaine went missing. Rose told Anne Marie that their mother, Rena, had come in the middle of the night to collect Charmaine.

Rose had actually murdered the young girl, and buried her in a coal pit in the cellar. Fred got out of jail in late July 1971, and helped Rose move the body to a new burial site in the garden. When the landlady of their Midland Road home asked Fred to build an extension on the home, he built the new kitchen over Charmaine's grave.

When her remains were found years later they exhibited telltale signs of Fred having been involved in her burial. Like Anna McFall before her, Charmaine's body was missing the kneecaps, and some fingers and toes. Fred kept these bones as trophies of his kills. Many of his later victims would also be found missing those bones. The various bones have never been found.

In August of 1971, Rena did come back to England to collect her children. She asked Fred's father where she could find him. Fred and Rena went to a local pub where Fred plied his wife with alcohol. He then molested her and strangled her to death in the back of his car. Rena was decapitated, dismembered, and buried in Letterbox Field. Her remains were not found until Fred's confession over twenty years later.

On January 29th, 1972, Fred and Rose got married. Rose said of their wedding, "I had to beg [Fred] to take off his overalls. His brother John witnessed the marriage, and another friend of Fred's who had so many aliases he had to scribble out the first name he wrote on the certificate."

Fred signified himself as a bachelor on the marriage certificate, which Rose did not object to. Some have pointed to this as evidence that Rose knew Fred's first wife, Rena, was already dead.

Fred's brother John not only helped the two get married; he also allegedly began aiding the couple in their horrific crimes. John would often have sex with Rose, and rape Anna Marie and a younger West child. He also used his job to help Fred and Rose cover up their murders. John was a garbage man, and would allegedly allow the couple to dispose of body parts, or victims' possessions in his truck, to avoid the suspicions of the neighbors, and the local sanitary workers.

25 Cromwell Street

Rose was pregnant with the couple's second child when they got married. The growing West family decided they needed more room to live. Fred, Rose, Anne Marie, and Heather, moved to 25 Cromwell Street, in Gloucester. Charmaine's absence was not yet conspicuous. On June 1st of the same year, Rose gave birth to their second biological daughter, Mae.

Fred converted the large house into several rental apartments and bedsits. There could have been up to 30 people living there at any given time. The house was not a good neighborhood. Shaun Boyle, the boyfriend of a former lodger said 25 Cromwell was "well known as a place where drifters and dropouts and teenagers who had been kicked out of home could look for bedsits. You'd never question it if someone moved on."

Rose began doing sex work out of one of the rooms under the name Mandy, the same pseudonym Rena used. Fred installed peep holes into the room where she worked so he could watch his wife sleep with other men. Bill Letts, Rose's father, would often come to the makeshift brothel and have sex with his own daughter.

In October of 1972, the Wests found a woman hitchhiking. Seventeen year old Caroline Owens took a ride from the Wests, and agreed to be their live-in nanny. Caroline was immediately uncomfortable in the house. Fred and Rose would constantly ask her about her sex life, and insist she and her boyfriend use their bed for sex. Fred also claimed he could perform abortions and promised to help her if she ever "got into trouble."

Caroline quit the nanny job and left the house. A few weeks later she was picked up by the Wests again while hitchhiking.

Caroline was bound in the van, and Rose began to assault her before they even made it back to the house. She said "[Fred] stopped the car, turned around in the seat and punched me until I was knocked out. I was tied up and my mouth was taped. They sneaked me into the house, and it was 12 hours of sexual assault. Mostly by Rose." She said her experience with Rose was much more disturbing than her experience with Fred. She felt "utterly degraded".

Before Caroline got out of Cromwell Road, Fred threatened her that he would "bury [her] under the paving stones of Gloucester", and implied that there were "hundreds of girls" already there. She was only able to escape after she agreed to be the children's nanny again.

She, Rose, and two of the girls took a trip to the laundromat. Rose ran into a tenant of 25 Cromwell and, while she was distracted by conversation, Caroline ran.

Caroline filed charges against Fred and Rose but did not push a rape charge. She didn't want everyone knowing her personal business, and her step-father was worried about the neighbors gossiping about their family. Fred and Rose were found guilty of the lesser charge of indecent assault. They were both charged the measly sum of £50.

Caroline believed for years that she was the reason Fred and Rose began killing their victims, and blamed her for the subsequent deaths of the other women. She said, "After it came out, I felt terribly emotional and guilty. I thought I'd been selfish because my first thought was to protect myself, even though the Wests' behavior had been suspicious - I didn't want people to probe into my life. If I had really persisted, the police would at least have been watching Fred. And, on the flip side, if I hadn't said anything at all, would the women still have been alive? Because I caused a fuss Fred and Rose no longer trusted the women they abused, and so eradicated their fears by killing them."

Of course Caroline was not to blame for any of the crimes the ghoulish pair would later commit. Both Wests had already killed separately, and nothing would stop them from doing it again, together. Stephen West, the pair's first son, blames a shoddy system for his parents' further crimes. He said, "All they got was a fine. It was like a green light. You know, go for it."

Just a few weeks after the trial for Caroline's abuse, the couple began a horrific string of murders that would eventually give 25

Cromwell Street the nickname The House of Horrors.

Nineteen year old Lynda Gough was the first victim the Wests killed together. Lynda was a seamstress who was having multiple affairs with lodgers at 25 Cromwell Street, and who the pair asked to be the children's nanny. As a result she had become acquainted with Fred and Rose. The three ended up sharing a bed together on several occasions. On April 19th, 1973 she left home abruptly and did not return.

Her mother began asking around the neighborhood for clues as to where her daughter may have gone. Her search led her to the Cromwell Street house. She knocked on the door and asked Rose where her daughter was. Rose made a show of attempting to remember Lynda, and then told Mrs. Gough the girl had briefly stayed with them, but had moved to Weston-super-Mare. Mrs. Gough noticed Rose was wearing items of Lynda's clothing, including her slippers, and that there were more of her belongings hanging on the washing line.

Lynda had not moved away. Rose was wearing a dead girl's clothes. Fred and Rose had killed Lynda, dismembered her body, and buried her in the floor beneath their bathroom. When her body was found over 20 years later it appeared her head had been wrapped in a tape mask fitted with breathing tubes placed in her nostrils to briefly keep her alive while they tortured her.

Investigators also found string and rope buried with her body. Fred later admitted he liked to string his victims up from the beams on the cellar ceiling.

Lynda most likely died of suffocation or strangulation. Her body was missing kneecaps and some fingers, a trademark of Fred West.

The Wests next victim was 15-year-old Carol Ann Cooper. She was living in Pine's Children's Home in Worcester. On November 10th, 1973, Carol was waiting at a bus stop, heading home after seeing a movie with her boyfriend. She was most likely pushed into Fred's van and bound there before being smuggled into the house, similar to the abduction of Caroline Roberts.

She was also hung from the cellar ceiling, assaulted, and murdered. She was decapitated, her body was dismembered, and she buried under the cellar floor.

Just one month after Carol Ann Cooper, the Wests targeted Lucy Partington. Lucy was a 21-year-old Exeter University student who was visiting home for Christmas vacation. She left a friend's house at 10:15 on December 27th, 1973, and was never seen by her friends or family again.

Lucy was also decapitated and buried under the floor of the cellar. It is believed that the Wests kept her alive for several days before killing her. Lucy's body was found buried with the knife that was used to dismember her.

On January 3rd, 1974, Fred admitted himself to the hospital with a serious laceration on his right hand that required several stitches. The wound was consistent with the size, shape, and depth of a wound one might get if injured with the knife found with Lucy's body. Investigators believe Fred sustained the injury while dismembering Lucy.

In April 1974 the couple picked up Therese Siegenthaler, a Swiss student who was studying sociology at Greenwich Community College, and was attempting to hitchhike across England. She, too, ended up buried in the cellar. Fred and Rose mistook her Swiss accent for a Dutch one, and would refer to her as Tulip.

Their next killing also took place that year. Fifteen year old Shirley Hubbard went missing in November of 1974. She was a foster child who was attending a work experience program. Shirley was abducted at a bus stop while on the way home from a date with her boyfriend. Her body was found in the cellar with a tape mask and a breathing tube similar to that of Lynda Gough's.

Brian Leveson, the lawyer for the prosecution, explained the purpose of the tape masks during the West's trial, "The breathing tube or tubes demonstrate that Shirley must have been alive when the mask was applied. Its purpose can only have been to keep her wholly under control, unable to see, unable to cry out, just able to breathe."

They wanted utter control of the victim while they tortured and abused her.

In April of 1975 Fred and Rose killed the last woman who would be buried in the cellar. Eighteen-year-old Juanita Mott was a former lodger at 25 Cromwell, who then moved out to live with friends. While hitchhiking along B4215 Juanita was picked up by the Wests and taken back to Cromwell Road. She was also decapitated and dismembered before being buried under the floor in the cellar.

After Fred buried Juanita the killer couple ran out of room in the cellar to hide the bodies of their victims. Fred poured concrete over the graves, and made the torture chamber into another room in the house, where his oldest daughters would sleep.

There are no known murders between Juanita in April 1975 and their next murder in 1978, but the couple hadn't reformed in those few years. During the trial years later an anonymous woman, simply known as Miss A, came forward saying she escaped Fred and Rose at the height of their killing spree.

In 1977, when Miss A was 15 years old, she ran away from an area children's home, and ended up at Cromwell. She befriended the Wests and, when she decided to run away again, she went to them. She said she was taken to a room where she was confronted with two other girls, who were both, naked. Rose stripped and assaulted her, and Fred raped her.

Oddly, Fred and Rose let Miss a go. Considering their compulsion for torture and murder, as well as all they had to lose by having the police investigate them, it seems strange that they would let a potential murder victim--and potential informant--go free.

During the trial, Leveson said the Wests, "obviously made an assessment that this girl would not go to the police." Still, it was a dangerous move that was probably born of their growing arrogance.

Some suggest that the Wests may have found young girls who were allowing them to act out their sexually fantasies with them, so the kidnappings and rapes slowed down.

Others think the couple was still killing, and just buried them somewhere other than 25 Cromwell. Author Geoffrey Wansell, writer of the in depth biography of the Wests, An Evil Love: The Life of Frederick West, said, "Serial killers don't stop until they are caught. There cannot be much doubt that Fred and Rosemary carried on killing after they had buried all those remains in Cromwell Street. Almost certainly they found other places to dispose of victims".

Wansell has also claimed, "I would not be surprised if there were more than 90."

In April 1977 an 18-year-old woman named Shirley Robinson came to stay at 25 Cromwell. She began an affair with Fred and became pregnant by him. Rose was also pregnant by a client at the time. Rose used to brag to the neighbors that Shirley was pregnant with her husband's child.

Investigators believe that the novelty of this affair grew tired for Rose, and she began to be threatened by Shirley's relationship with Fred. Fred, too, was allegedly tired of Shirley. He told his brother-in-law, Jim-Tyler, "She wants to get between me and Rose. She wants Rose out so she can take over and take her place. I'm not having that, she's got to fucking go."

When she was 8 months pregnant, Shirley was murdered, dismembered and decapitated. Unlike the other women, she was buried in the garden at 25 Cromwell.

After her death, Rose attempted to claim a maternity benefit from Social Services in Shirley's name.

In August 1979 the Wests invited 16-year-old Alison Chambers to be their live-in nanny. She was a runaway from a local children's home, who was actually still in touch with her family, who, presumably simply didn't have the means to take care of her. Alison was the second victim to be buried in a garden grave.

In order to make it seem like Alison had simply moved away, Fred and Rose posted a letter to Alison's mother that she had written before they murdered her. They sent it from a Northamptonshire postbox that was approximately a 2 hour drive from Gloucester.

Between 1974 and 1980 Rose had had six more children, two of whom were conceived with one of her Jamaican clients. The West family now consisted of Fred, Rose, Anne Marie, Mae, Heather, Stephen, Tara, Rosemary, Lucyanna, Louise, and Barry.

The West siblings were being constantly terrorized by their parents. Rose's brother, Graham Letts said, "Whenever we (he and his wife) walked into the house there was never any noise. Even with nine or ten children around, you could hear a pin drop...It reminded me in some ways of our mom. Rosie was every bit as strict, and seemed to be using the same tactics: 'If you don't do as I say, you'll regret it.'"

Heather West

Just as Rose's brother suspected, Rose and her husband were indeed severely abusing their children. They were all savagely beaten for reasons Rosemary would fabricate. Stephen recalls an incident where his mother called him home from school to tie him up and beat him for something his sister had actually done.

If the children weren't being abused they were being ignored. They were completely in charge of their own upbringing, having to do all their own cooking and cleaning from the time they were seven years old.

Anne Marie was not only physically abused. Fred would sexually abuse her daily from the time she was ten. She said, "I was told I should be grateful and that I was lucky I had such caring parents who thought of me...My father's abuse continued without a break until I ran away from home at fifteen."

At fifteen Anne Marie discovered she was pregnant by her father. The pregnancy ended up being ectopic, wherein the embryo attaches to the fallopian tube wall, instead of the uterus, and Anne Marie had an abortion.

She moved in with her boyfriend, Christopher Davis. The young couple was running low on funds, and was forced to move into the West home for a brief period. Christopher noticed how tense the house made Anne Marie, and how strangely disconnected from reality Heather acted. The two girls confided in him everything that their parents had done to them.

Christopher said he would confront the Wests on behalf of the girls, but Anne Marie begged him not to saying, "For Christ's sake doesn't, because they'll kill us both."

Anne Marie and Christopher moved out again and started a family. Heather asked to live with them but, as she was not yet 16--the age she would be allowed to legally leave home--Anne Marie knew Fred and Rose would make sure Heather ended up back at 25 Cromwell with them.

When Anne Marie left home, Fred turned his attentions to Mae and Heather. He refused to let them lock the door while they showered, and would come into their bathroom to fondle them while they were naked. The girls began standing guard for each other while the other one showered, in an attempt to avoid their father's abuse.

Fred also installed a peep hole in their bedroom, and would watch them change. They had no privacy, and no refuge from the constant abuse. Heather used to talk about running away and living a peaceful life in the Forest of Dean.

Heather took the abuse the worst. Mae said, "She was so miserable, but she never talked about it. She just became a loner and a bit of a recluse." She would alternate between being totally despondent, and being aggressive. She would rarely even socialize with her own siblings. When the family would visit Anne Marie, Heather would stand alone at the edge of the yard, and not speak to anyone.

She was the same at school. Although she was a good student, some staff recognized that Heather experienced severe mood swings. One of her teachers described her as, "Jekyll and Hyde. One minute nice as pie and the next very aggressive."

Heather's teachers also noticed that she refused to change or shower after physical activity. After she was forced to shower, her friend Denise Harrison noticed that Heather was covered in bruises and sores.

Heather confided in Denise that she was being abused by her parents. Rumors about the West household began swirling. Heather admitted most of the rumors were true. One of her classmates told their parents, who were friends of the Wests. They told Fred that Heather had been gossiping about their family.

Anne Marie said, "Fred and Rose were furious that Heather had been discussing their business outside the family, and she suffered a tremendous beating." Fred also began escorting Heather to and from school, to further isolate her from the outside world.

Denise told her parents about what Heather told her, but they also knew the Wests and didn't believe they were capable of such horrors. If someone had followed up and tried to protect Heather, maybe what happened next could have been prevented.

Anne Marie wrote, "I remember the last time I saw Heather; I even recall what she was wearing. She had on a baggy white T-shirt and leggings. Her dark brown hair was very long and worn loose. I made a note of it in my diary which later helped the police pinpoint exactly when she went missing. The date was 17 June, 1987--my elder daughter Michelle's 3rd birthday."

The next day Heather received a rejection from a job she had applied to. She had finished school earlier that year and had begun applying to cleaning jobs at hotels in holiday towns. A job she had gotten in

Torque had fallen through at the last minute. Her dream of getting away from her parents had been crushed. Mae said she "cried all the way through the night."

On June 19th, Mae and Stephen saw Heather sitting sullenly on the couch before they left for school. By the time they got home Heather had disappeared. Fred told them she had actually gone to Torque to see if she could get the job.

Fred had actually strangled his daughter to death, dismembered and decapitated her, and placed her body parts in garbage bins to await a convenient time to bury her.

Anne Marie said, "Dad said it was early morning. He strangled her in the hallway.

He hot one of the black bins from the house, cut her legs and arms off, put her in the dustbin, put the lid on, and put her in the cupboard under the basement stairs. Then he said, we went to bed at 9pm, and he buried her in the garden."

Fred collected some of Heather's clothes and belongings in garbage bags, and put them in the trash cans of a neighborhood veterinary clinic. They would be taken away in the garbage collection, and it would look as though Heather had packed up and left. Stephen noticed his sister didn't take a book she had recently won that was her most prized possession.

Stephen says Fred made him dig his sister's grave under the presence that he was going to build a fish pond in their garden. "He told me 'I want a hole there, about four feet deep and six across, and I want you to lay blue plastic in the hole and leave it'".

A few days later the hole was filled in, and no fish pond was built. Fred had paved over the area with pink and yellow patio stones, and had built a barbeque pit adjacent to it. The family would have cookouts on Heather's grave.

In the following years, Fred and Rose told many stories of where Heather had gone. They said she had run away with a lesbian lover, and said she was probably working as a prostitute or drug dealer under an assumed name. When the other children grew concerned they hadn't heard from her,

Fred said they shouldn't involve the police, as Heather was wanted for credit card fraud, and she would get in trouble if they found her.

The Wests then began receiving phone calls from "Heather". The phone would ring and either Fred or Rose would pick it up, and have a conversation in front of the children with whoever was on the other end of the line. Of course the kids were never allowed to speak to whoever was pretending to be their sister. Sometimes Rose would even get into an argument with the fake Heather. Fred would also claim to have seen her in various places.

Between performances of pretending Heather was alive, Fred would threaten his other children that they'd "end up under the patio like Heather"

Rosemary allegedly changed significantly after Heather disappeared. Photos of Heather were removed from the home, the children were forbidden to speak of her, and Rose would spend hours alone sobbing.

Mae said her mother never hit her again after that point.

Investigation

In May 1992 Fred began sexually abusing one of his younger daughters, allegedly recording one of the rapes. The West daughter told a friend about what had happened to her.

In August 1992 the friend asked a police officer what to do if someone was being abused by their family. The officer alerted Social Services to the rumors about the West house. Authorities obtained a warrant to search 25 Cromwell Street for evidence of child pornography and child abuse.

On August 6th, 1992 Fred West was arrested and charged with rape and sodomy. Rose was arrested for child cruelty, and being an accomplice to her husband's sexual abuse. The five youngest children were taken from 25 Cromwell and put in care at Jordan's Brook Community Home.

They were extensively interviewed and given physical examinations. Evidence of physical and sexual abuse was clearly present. The children all explained the abuse they had suffered at the hands of their parents. The girls described how Fred would sexually abuse them, and Rose would tell them they were "asking for it" and that they deserved it.

Anne Marie heard her father had been arrested for abuse, but was maintaining his innocence. On August 7th, 1992 Anne Marie made an extensive statement to Constable

Savage about the abuse she suffered in the West house. She said, "I went through hell making that statement to Hazel. It brought back horrors I thought I had blocked out forever. It shook me to the core and left me traumatized."

She also told Constable Savage that she had been looking for her mother, Rena, and her half-sister, Charmaine, for years and had not been able to locate them.

On June 7th, 1993 the Wests were brought before Judge Gabriel Hutton. Fred was charged with three counts of rape and sodomy; Rose faced charges for "causing or encouraging the commission of unlawful sexual intercourse with a girl under the age of 16", and "cruelty to a child."

On the day of the trial the children refused to testify against their parents. The case against them collapsed, and Fred was allowed to return to live at 25 Cromwell.

Anne Marie also retracted the statement she made to the police. This may have been because of a phone call from her mother where she vaguely threatened her. Rose told Anne Marie, "If you think anything of me or your dad you'll keep your mouth shut." She feared what might happen if she angered Rose. Anne Marie also saw the distress the ordeal was causing her sister, and decided not to push it. She did, however, continue to ask for help in finding Rena and Charmaine.

Constable Savage, knowing Fred's dark past, continued to believe Anne Marie's statement was true. She would spend the next year searching for signs of Heather. British authorities decided to involve Interpol to see whether Heather had fled the country. No evidence of her existence was found.

The rest of the West children were still in foster care. Social workers began hearing them speak of a threat their father would frequently use against them when they were misbehaving. He told them they would "end up under the patio like Heather" if they didn't cooperate.

The police took the West children's statements regarding the patio at Cromwell, and used them to obtain a warrant to dig up the garden at the West family home. On

February 23rd, 1994, authorities began work excavating the Wests garden.

Rose called Fred at work and told him they were digging up the garden. Fred went to Gloucester Police Station to voluntarily give a statement; only his statement was completely false. He told Detective Constable Hazel Savage that he had seen Heather recently, in Birmingham.

He also said that she had most likely changed her name and become a prostitute, or was working with a drug cartel in Bahrain. Authorities did not yet have any reason to detain Fred, so he was allowed to return home.

Rose was interviewed separately at her home, but also maintained that she did not know where Heather was.

On February 25th, 1994, Detective Constables Savage and Law came to 25 Cromwell in order to collect information on the Wests family members, so that they could interview the extended family about Heather's disappearance.

Fred asked the detectives if he could be taken to the police station. In the car he confessed to Constable Savage that he had actually killed his daughter.

Fred said he choked Heather to death by accident after an argument about her moving out of the house. He told Savage, "I lunged at her...and grabbed her throat...and I held for a minute. How long I held her for I don't know, I can't remember...I can just remember lunging for her throat and the next minute she's gone blue. I looked at her and, I mean, I was shaking from head to foot, I mean, what the heck had gone wrong?"

Fred said his wife knew nothing of Heather's murder, but she was arrested on suspicion of murder anyway.

After taking his statement the detectives took Fred back to 25 Cromwell to point out where Heather's grave was.

Just one day after making a full confession, Fred retracted his statement about Heather's murder. He said, "Heather is not in the garden. Heather's alive and well...I have no idea what her name is, because I won't let her tell me. She contacts me when she's in this country...They can dig there for evermore. Nobody or nothing's under my patio."

Since obtaining the search warrant on February 24th, fifteen police officers had been working tirelessly in the rain to excavate the West's yard. On February 26th, after Fred had retracted his statement about Heather being buried in the garden, the search team found a femur belonging to an unknown person, and Heather West's skeleton. Heather had been dismembered and decapitated. She, like Fred's other victims, was missing a kneecap, and several finger and toe bones.

Fred re-confessed to Heather's murder. He was questioned about the other femur found in the garden, and was fairly straightforward with investigators. He said it probably belonged to Shirley Robinson, "the girl who caused the problem."

Fred then said Shirley's friend was buried somewhere in the garden, too. He admitted to strangling and killing Alison Chambers, who he could not identify by name. Rose was arrested on suspicion of the murder of Shirley Robinson, and an unknown female.

On February 27th, 1994 Fred was formally charged with Heather West's murder. He once again claimed that his wife knew nothing of his murders, and she was let out on bail.

Fred was assigned an appropriate adult, Janet Leach. An appropriate adult usually assists minors who have been brought in for questioning in understanding the legal proceedings. Due to Fred's illiteracy, he was also eligible for this service. Janet was a 38-year-old, divorced mother of five, who was working toward being a social worker.

Fred became quite taken with Janet. She was said to closely resemble Anna McFall, and some believed Fred was actually in love with her. Janet spent 400 hours with Fred over the short period she was assigned to his case.

Janet said she became a confidant of Fred's; he would only speak to the police when she was in the room, and he began to confess crimes to her that he would not admit to the police. He referred to her as his "only friend".

She said Fred was extremely blasé about his crimes. She said, "He showed no emotion. No pity. No remorse. We might have been discussing the weather."

Janet's confidentiality agreement prevented her from telling the police the horrific things Fred admitted to her when they were out of the room. The knowledge of his crimes weighed on Janet. She threatened to quit her position if Fred did not confess to the police.

On February 28th the remains of Shirley Robinson and her unborn child, and Alison Chambers were pulled from the ground at 25 Cromwell Road. The media had gotten a hold of the story, and people began coming forward asking if their missing loved ones had been found in the garden. Fred was asked about Lynda Gough after her family said she had been last seen around 25 Cromwell.

On March 4th, 1994 Fred made a full, handwritten confession stating "I, Frederick West, authorize my solicitor, Howard Ogden, to advise Superintendent Bennett that I wish to admit to a further (approx.) nine killings, expressly Charmaine, Rena, Lynda Gough, and others to be identified"

Fred confessed that there were five more bodies buried under the floor in the cellar, one more in the main floor bathroom, one under the kitchen at the Midland Road home, one in Fingerpost Field, and one in Letterbox Field.

He maintained Rose knew nothing of the murders. He also claimed that he never deliberately tortured or murdered anyone, saying, "Yeah, see, you've got the killing all wrong, no, nobody went through hell, enjoyment turned to disaster, well most of it anyway."

The condition of the bodies and testimony from surviving victims made it clear that a victim's time with the Wests was far from consensual, and the murders were not simply sadistic sex acts that accidently went too far.

Fred allegedly admitted to Stephen that his victims were missing fingers, toes, and kneecaps because he would remove them as a form of torture while the victim was still alive.

Fred was again taken back to Cromwell to point out where the other graves were. On March 5th, Therese Siegenthaler and Shirley Hubbard were found, and Fred was taken to Letterbox Field to point out Rena's burial place. Lucy Partington and Juanita Mott were found on the 6th.

On the 7th Lynda Gough was found, and Fred was taken to Fingerpost Field to point out Anna McFall's grave. Fred never admitted to killing Anna, and always claimed she was the love of his life. He had no explanation, though, for how he knew she was dead, or how he knew where she was buried.

Carol Ann Cooper was found on March 8th. Police obtained a search warrant for 25 Midland Road, and Charmaine's remains were found there on May 4th.

Trial

On June 30th, 1994, Fred and Rosemary West were brought to court to be jointly charged for the murders of the women found in their home. Rose was to be sentenced for nine of the murders, and Fred was to face sentencing for eleven.

Fred attempted to make contact with his wife, reaching out to touch her and speak in her ear. Rose publicly rebuffed him, and recoiled at his touch. This angered and embarrassed Fred, who then retracted his statements that Rose knew nothing of the murders.

Anna McFall's body had been found in Fingerpost Field on June 7th, but she had not been positively identified until after the June 30th hearing. Fred was charged with the murder of Anna McFall on July 3rd, 1994.

A little after noon, on January 1st, 1995, while awaiting trial and sentencing for all 12 known murders, Fred West committed suicide by hanging in his cell at Winson Green Prison, Birmingham. He had allegedly created a suicide kit consisting of bed sheets, razor blades, and a cotton reel, that was found six days after he entered the prison. It was not confiscated. Seven months later Fred used it to take his own life.

Fred's suicide note read:

"To Rose West, Steve and Mae,

Well Rose it's your birthday on 29 November 1994 and you will be 41 and still beautiful and still lovely and I love you. We will always be in love. The most wonderful thing in my life was when I met you. Our love is special to us. So, love, keep your promises to me. You know what they are. Where we are put together for ever and ever is up to you. We loved Heather, both of us. I would love Charmaine to be with Heather and Rena. You will always be Mrs. West, all over the world. That is important to me and to you. I haven't got you a present, but all I have is my life. I will give it to you, my darling. When you are ready, come to me. I will be waiting for you."

At the bottom of his note he had drawn a headstone with the words "In loving memory. Fred West. Rose West. Rest in peace where no shadow falls. In perfect peace he waits for Rose, his wife" written on it.

Rose said of her husband's suicide "I am so relieved. He was evil. He should have died long ago."

Even after the questioning had finished, Janet Leach continued to visit and write to Fred. She was allegedly devastated at the loss of Fred. Her son, Paul, said she "fell under West's spell" and she was deeply affected by his suicide. It does seem as though the two shared a special bond.

Rose had gone through six different appropriate adults during her questionings.

They couldn't stand to listen to the details of what went on at 25 Cromwell. Janet, though, was present for almost every questioning, additional confession, and continued to visit Fred after her role as appropriate adult had finished.

Janet claims she was not upset at his loss, but frustrated and upset that he died with more secrets. She said Fred had told her there were twenty more bodies to be found. Janet said, "I was desperate. I couldn't sleep at night. I kept having nightmares about those poor girls in the cellar. But I felt I had to keep talking to Fred. Otherwise, how would their families know what had happened to them?"

Fred was cremated on March 29th, 1995. A service was held which only Tara, Stephen, and Mae attended. Other families having funerals that day were outraged that their loved one had to share a funeral date and place with Fred West.

The service only lasted five minutes. It was an unsentimental, borderline hostile affair where Fred was not remembered fondly. Reverend Smith told the West children present that they should, "remember everyone else who has also suffered because of these tragic events."

Fred West's ashes were scattered at the Welsh seaside resort he named his son after, Barry Island; a place he visited as a child, and as a father with his own children.

After Fred recanted his statement that Rose didn't know anything of the killings, Rose was also charged with Charmaine's murder, bringing her count up to ten.

Rose's trial began on October 3rd, 1995. During the seven weeks of evidence, the jury heard from former tenants of 25 Cromwell Road, Anne Marie West, Caroline Owens, Miss A--the anonymous woman who Fred and Rose assaulted in 1977--, and Rose's own family members.

Rose herself made the choice to testify in her own trial, against the advice of her counsel. She opened her statements by attempting to set herself up as another one of Fred's victims. She said, "He had promised me the world, promised me everything and because

I was so young I fell for his lies but because I was so young I did not realize they were lies at the time. He promised to love me and care for me and I fell for it."

Rose attempted to claim Fred did not let her in the cellar where several of the murders took place, and where most of the bodies were found. She said he would lock the door and do his business in secret. Those who survived Rose's abuse know this is far from the truth. Even Fred alluded to Rose being the more sexually aggressive one of the pair.

Detective Superintendent John Bennett, the Senior Investigating Officer on the case said, "The whole case was about Rosemary being sexually insatiable. There were huge quantities of pornographic material and sex objects in the house. I firmly believe that Rose murdered the girls and Fred disposed of the bodies."

Rose did herself no favors on the stand. She laughed and joked during her testimony, and told blatant lies. After being shown photographs of her victims she said she didn't remember six of the ten women she was being charged with murdering.

Of the assault on Caroline Owens, which was known to be an aggressive assault largely perpetrated by Rose, she said, "As soon as she put up resistance, as soon as I realized that she was against this, that she did not agree with it in any way I stopped. All I can remember is being very frightened. Fred was a threat at this moment in time. I was pleading with Fred all the time for it to stop. I didn't want to get involved in anything like this. I didn't want Caroline to get hurt. It was just a mess."

Rose only became somewhat emotional when Heather was brought up. However, many believe her tears were just an act.

Janet Leach, Fred's appropriate adult, testified that she had become a confidant of Fred's and that he had told her Rose "played a major part" in all the murders. She said Fred had told her the murders were largely "Rose's mistakes" where an act of sexual sadism went too far, and the victim ended up dead.

Janet testified that Fred had confided in her about a pact between him and Rose where he would take full responsibility for all the murders.

Janet also lied under oath about having sold her story to the press. She had actually sold her account of her friendship with Fred to the Daily Mirror for £100,000.

Janet had been experiencing severe health problems because of her involvement with Fred West, and her exclusive knowledge of many of his crimes. While she was testifying on the stand at Rose's trial, Janet collapsed. She had had a stroke.

The trial was halted for six days while Janet recovered. When she returned to the stand she confessed she had lied about selling her story.

The trial ended on November 16th, 1995. On November 21st, the jury found Rose guilty of the murder of Charmaine West, Heather West, and Shirley Robinson. The next day, the jury found Rose guilty of the murders of the remaining seven women: Lynda Gough, Carol Ann Cooper, Lucy Partington, Therese Siegenthaler, Shirley Hubbard, Juanita Mott, and Alison Chambers.

The judge sentenced Rose to life in prison with the recommendation that she never be let out. He called her crimes "appalling and depraved".

A life sentence in England at the time did not actually mean a person would spend the remainder of their life in prison. It meant they would serve a minimum of 15 years before parole would be entertained. The Lord Chief Justice declared Rosemary should spend at least 25 years in prison.

Rose continued to protest her innocence. Barry West has said, "My mum continually lies about her involvement in the hopes that one day she'll be free, but she knows every detail of what took place."

On July 1997, Home Secretary Jack Straw gave Rose a life tariff, ensuring she would never get out of prison. Rose allegedly became close friends with Myra Hindley, another woman who had committed serial murders with her partner, and one of the only other women in UK history to be serving a whole life tariff.

Aftermath

25 Cromwell Street

On October 7th, 1996, Gloucester City Council began demolition of the House of Horrors at 25 Cromwell Street. The council had bought the house and the adjoining vacant lot for £40,000. The money from the sale went to the solicitor who was dealing with Fred West's estate. It was used to set up a trust for the five youngest West children.

Dismantling the house took 15 days. It was destroyed completely to avoid souvenir seekers getting a piece of the horrific history. The bricks were removed one-by-one, crushed, mixed with other materials, and used in undisclosed projects. The wood beams were all burned. The rivets and other metal were all melted. The foundations were filled in and capped with two feet of concrete.

A concrete pathway is all that exists on the lot now.

The West children

The five youngest West children were still in care when their father committed suicide and their mother went to prison for life. Tara, Barry, and Louise still live in Gloucester. Lucyanna and Rosemary Jr moved to the south of England

Anne Marie attempted suicide several times during her life. In 1999 she threw herself from a Gloucester bridge into the water below, and was carried quite a distance down river. She was pulled from the water, barely alive, by fire fighters.

She made a heartbreaking statement about her attempts to end her life, "People say I am lucky to have survived, but I wish I had died. I can still taste the fear. Still feel the pain."

As part of her healing process Anne Marie wrote a book about her childhood called Out of the Shadows: Fred West's Daughter Tells Her Harrowing Story of Survival.

Her partner Phil Davies has said, "Life has been a nightmare for Anne Marie, because she keeps reliving the trauma. What she's been through is unimaginably hard for anyone to cope with, but I'm so proud of her. It's a heavy burden, but she's just trying to lead an ordinary life now. With me and the kids supporting her, I think she can see a light at the end of the tunnel."

At Anne Marie's request, her mother, Rena, and her half-sister, Charmaine, were buried in the same coffin.

Stephen West also attempted suicide in January 2002, by hanging. Like his sister, he survived.

In December 2004, Stephen went to prison for 9 months for inappropriate sexual relations with a fourteen year old girl.

Stephen lamented "There's a bit of my dad in me."

At his trial Stephen's barrister, Stephen Mooney, said, "He had one of the most traumatic and distressing childhoods one can imagine, and what happened affected his emotional development. Anyone who had suffered like him had a tendency to remain emotionally less well-developed for his age."

Stephen co-wrote a book with his sister, Mae, about their experiences called Inside 25 Cromwell Street: The Terrifying True Story of a Life with Fred and Rose West.

Mae attempted to hide her identity. She changed her last name, and had plastic surgery to remove a distinctive mole from her face. She dropped off the radar and didn't speak out for 17 years, until 2011 when she said she realized, "Not talking doesn't make it go away". Mae says she has forgiven her parents.

Stephen, Tara, and Mae had a proper funeral for Heather on December 19th, 1995. It was held at St. Michael's parish church at Tintern, near the Forest of Dean where Heather always dreamed of running away to live. Rose wanted to be allowed to attend, but was not granted permission to leave prison for the service.

The other West

Fred's brother, John hanged himself in his garage on November 28th, 1996. During police questioning Fred said John aided him and his wife in disposing of evidence of their murders. At the time of his death he was awaiting a decision from a trial where he faced rape charges. Anne Marie reported that her uncle raped her over 300 times while she lived at 25 Cromwell Street. He would also go to the house to have sex with Rosemary.

There is no solid evidence linking John to his brother's murders but, considering his rape charges, and close relationship with his brother, it is certainly possible that those rumors are true.

Other notable people

Caroline Owens wrote two books on her experiences with the Wests: The Lost Girl: How I Triumphed Over Life at the Mercy of Fred and Rose West, and The One That Got Away: My Life Living With Fred and Rose West, which she co-wrote with Stephen Richards.

Caroline continued to have survivor's guilt for the rest of her life. She regretted her decision to not pursue the rape charge against the Wests. She did say, though, that the ordeal gave her a "backbone of steel" and a zest for life she didn't previously have. She said, "You can't keep being the victim. I always used to feel jinxed, like nothing would ever go right for me. Now I have such a zest for life and if I put my mind to something I can do whatever I want."

Caroline died in 2016 after a battle with cancer. Before she died she said she had forgiven Rose West for the horrific abuse.

Marian Partington says she also forgives Rose for murdering her sister, Lucy. She wrote to Rose in prison saying, "I do not feel any hostility towards you, just a deep sadness that all this happened and that your heart could not feel a truth that I wish you could know."

Rose allegedly rejected this forgiveness. Marian received a letter from the prison asking her to "please cease all correspondence, she does not wish to receive any further letters from you". Rose continues to maintain that she is innocent of the murder of Lucy Partington, and of the other nine murders she was charged with.

Marian wrote a book about the loss of her sister and the nature of forgiveness called If You Sit Very Still.

Terry Crick, a former neighbor and friend of Fred, was found dead in his car in January 1996, only a few weeks after he had testified in Rose's trial. Terry had gone to the police in 1970 to report Fred for performing illegal abortions. Terry said Fred had shown him the tools he used to do the procedures, and pictures of women's genitals he had taken after performing the procedure. Fred had wanted Terry to help him find women who needed his services.

Crick's widow, Janet Bates, said, "Terry had been shown disturbing images and went straight to the police but when they didn't do anything he felt responsible."

Terry alleged that Fred was a police informant, and that many officers were actually clients of Rose's. He believed the police had an interest in keeping Fred and Rose on the streets, so they never followed up on his tips, and turned a blind eye to their suspicious behavior.

Janet also says he told her that he had made a full statement to the police after Fred's arrest, but that parts of it were missing when it was read back to him in court at Rose's trial. After the trial he said, "Now Rose has been found guilty I can perhaps give a sigh of relief, but I am sure that there are more bodies."

The stress of the trial, the nagging thought that he was somehow responsible for the murders that happened after his tip was ignored, and his certainty that there were more victims yet to be found led Terry to take his own life by carbon monoxide poisoning.

Conclusion

The effect of Fred and Rosemary West has been far-reaching and devastating. The House of Horrors at 25 Cromwell Street has been totally obliterated, but it will not be as easy to erase the memories of what went on there. The lives of at least twelve people ended, horrifically, and far too soon, at the hands of the Wests. The families of the victims must now attempt to pick up the pieces of their shattered lives and find a way to move on.

Marian Partington has been working toward forgiveness of the Wests since her sister's body was uncovered at 25 Cromwell. She has worked with The Forgiveness Project, an organization that helps people who have suffered through various painful experiences attempt to change their rage and want for revenge into "a quest for restoration and healing."

Her story on The Forgiveness Project website states, "...my work has been about connecting with Rosemary West's humanity and refusing to go down the far easier and more predictable path of demonizing her. I take every opportunity to talk about her as a human being."

People who do bad things are no less human than the rest of us. Demonizing them and wanting them to suffer through the same pain as their victims essentially makes you no better than them. The only way to move forward and find peace with a situation, however horrific, is to find a way to forgive.

Marian concludes her Forgiveness Project story with, "Some people have asked whether I feel I'm betraying Lucy by doing this and I say, 'No, absolutely the opposite: I feel I'm honoring Lucy by lining myself up for forgiveness.'"

44976375R00148

Printed in Poland
by Amazon Fulfillment
Poland Sp. z o.o., Wrocław